ICE HOCKEY MADE SIMPLE:
A SPECTATOR'S GUIDE

FOURTH EDITION

by P.J. Harari and Dave Ominsky

Illustrated by Anna Mendoza and Stephen J. Lattimer

Cover design by Eugene Cheltenham

Photographs © by Bruce Bennett Studios

2009 Reprint
© 2002, 1998, 1996, 1993 First Base Sports, Inc.,
Los Angeles, California

http://www.firstbasesports.com

Look for these other Spectator Guides:

- Basketball Made Simple
- Football Made Simple
- Soccer Made Simple

2009 Reprint
© 2002, 1998, 1996, 1993 First Base Sports, Inc.,
Los Angeles, California

ISBN-13: 978-1-884309-11-3
ISBN-10: 1-884309-11-9
Library of Congress Catalog Card Number: 2002091855

We welcome your comments and questions:
FIRST BASE SPORTS, INC.
P.O. BOX 1731
MANHATTAN BEACH, CALIFORNIA 90267-1731
U.S.A.
E-mail: feedback@firstbasesports.com

Typesetting by Jelico Graphics

HOW TO USE THIS BOOK

The sport of hockey has become vastly more popular over the past decade due in part to the National Hockey League's expansion into the Southern and Western U.S. This fast-paced, electrifying sport has always appealed to fans both young and old wherever it was played across the U.S. and Canada, and today more new fans are discovering the thrill than ever before. The excitement has even extended to the sport of roller hockey which has attracted great youth participation and spurred the birth of professional roller hockey leagues. These many new fans need a resource to assist them in better understanding this great sport.

This book aims to educate anyone who wants to know more about the exciting game of ice hockey. It is written for use by a variety of audiences — adults who want to become fans, children who want to learn the basics of the sport they are playing and even existing fans who want a quick reference guide to their favorite sport.

Each chapter has been written to stand alone, so you do not have to sit and read the book from cover to cover. However, the chapters do build on each other, so if you start at page 1 and read through to the end, the chapters flow logically and become more detailed as you progress.

This book will mainly discuss the rules of ice hockey as played at the professional level in the United States. Rules, as well as any word or phrase printed in *italics*, can be referenced quickly and easily using the book's glossary or index. So get ready to learn about ice hockey, America's most exciting sport.

HOCKEY ORGANIZATIONS

PROFESSIONAL MAJOR LEAGUE

National Hockey League (NHL): Organized in 1917, the NHL has grown to 30 teams divided into 2 *conferences* (with 3 *divisions* each). Currently, 6 of its teams are in Canada and the rest are in the United States. Since 1998, the league has added 4 *expansion teams*, 2 of which are in non-traditional hockey markets in the Southeastern U.S. Its teams play an 82-game *regular season* from October to April, then *playoffs* to compete for the *Stanley Cup*.

PROFESSIONAL MINOR LEAGUES

Eight professional *minor leagues* with a total of about 150 teams play in cities throughout the U.S. and Canada, helping to develop North America's best hockey talent. The *AHL* is considered the top-level development league for the NHL with its players moving directly to and from NHL rosters as needed throughout the year. The *International Hockey League (IHL)*, perhaps the most popular minor league throughout the 1990s and on the same development level as the AHL, folded in 2001 amid financial difficulties. Several of the other leagues—the *ECHL, CHL, UHL* and *WCHL*—are considered to be a step removed from the NHL, developing players mainly for the AHL. Many of these minor league teams are NHL "affiliates" which means that when their best players move up to the NHL ranks, they generally join the NHL team with which they are affiliated.

Each of these minor leagues follows its own set of rules, although most rules are similar to those followed by the NHL. One exception is the use by many of the minor leagues of a *shootout* instead of *overtime* to resolve *ties*. Some leagues use a combination of overtime *period*(s) followed by a shootout. A shootout is when teams alternate turns taking *penalty shots* at a *goal* defended by the opposing *goalie*. A different player must take each shot until a team runs out of players. The winner is the team that has the most *goals* after 5 shots are taken by each team (some leagues grant 3 shots each). If the game is still *tied* (each team has scored on an equal number of shots), the shootout continues with alternating penalty shots until one team scores and the other team does not.

American Hockey League (AHL): This is the top developmental league where all NHL clubs develop their top prospects – about 70% of NHL players spent some time in the AHL developing their skills. When the IHL folded in 2001, the AHL admitted 6 of its teams, growing to a total of 28 teams (5 in its Canadian Division and the rest in the U.S.) Teams play an 80-game season followed by *playoffs* where they compete for the Calder Cup. The AHL does not use a shootout system to resolve *ties*, instead using the same rules as the NHL. During the *regular season*, teams play a single 5-minute *sudden-death overtime period* with only 4 *skaters* (and one goalie) per side; this reduction of one player for overtime was first used in the AHL in 1998, a year before it was adopted by the NHL. If the teams still remain tied afterwards, the game is declared a tie. During the playoffs 20-minute sudden-death overtime periods are played until a goal is scored.

AHL teams carry a maximum of 19 players on their *rosters*, and to keep an emphasis on player development, no more than 7 may have over 260 games of combined NHL, AHL, IHL, and European elite league experience. Founded in 1936, the AHL is headquartered in Springfield, Massachusetts. The league surpassed 5 million in season attendance for the first time in 2002.

East Coast Hockey League (ECHL): Founded in 1988, the ECHL is the largest developmental hockey league in North America for players, coaches, *officials*, and front-office talent. Its 27 teams (growing to 29 in 2003-04) span over a dozen states stretching from New Orleans to South Florida to Trenton, NJ, to Peoria, IL. After a 72-game season that begins in mid-October, *playoffs* begin in early April with teams competing for the Kelly Cup, named after the league's only commissioner and founding father Pat Kelly. The ECHL uses a shootout system to resolve ties only during the regular season and only if the game remains tied after a single 5-minute overtime period. During the *playoffs* 20-minute sudden-death overtime periods are played until a goal is scored. Each team can carry up to 20 players on its roster and total payroll is limited by a *salary cap* to $9,250 per week ($462 per player average). To maintain the league's competitive balance and keep an emphasis on developing players, each team is limited to a maximum of 4 *veteran* players (those who have played 240 or more professional games). The ECHL is headquartered in Princeton, New Jersey.

Central Hockey League (CHL): The original CHL, started in 1963, became defunct in 1984. Re-formed in 1992, this league operated for 9 years before merging with the Western Professional Hockey League (WPHL) in 2001. The new entity, formed with the strongest franchises from each league (6 from the CHL and 10 from the WPHL), plays today under the CHL brand and is headquartered in Scottsdale, Arizona. Teams are generally located in the South Central U.S., stretching from New Mexico to Louisiana, with several in Texas. After a 64-game regular season that opens in late October, 8 teams go to the President's Cup playoffs in late March. To resolve tie games during the regular season, teams play a single 5-minute overtime period followed, if needed, by a 3-shot shootout to break the tie. In the playoffs, teams play successive 20-minute sudden-death overtime periods until a goal is scored.

Team rosters are limited to 18 players and must operate under a combined salary cap of $8,500 per week ($472 per player average). League rules limit the number of veteran players on a team (who have played in 230 or more professional games) to 5 and also require that at least 3 players be *rookies*.

United Hockey League (UHL): Formerly the Colonial Hockey League until 1997, the UHL plays a 76-game season that lasts from October to March. The league consists of 10 teams (growing to 11 in 2003-04) in 6 states from Michigan to Missouri and from Pennsylvania to New York. To maintain balance among teams, league rules require each team to have at least 3 rookies but no more than 6 veterans on its roster. The UHL is headquartered in Lake Saint Louis, Missouri.

West Coast Hockey League (WCHL): Established in 1995 and based in Ontario, California, the WCHL has 8 teams that compete in two divisions—a Northern Division with teams stretching from Alaska to Colorado, and a Southern Division with teams only in California. Its 74-game season starts in October and culminates in the Taylor Cup playoffs in April. Although league rules limit each team's salary total to just $12,000 per week, players are often "called up" to play in the more prestigious AHL during the season. To maintain competitive balance, league rules limit the number of veteran players on the team (who have played 280 or more professional games) to 8 and also require that at least 8 other players be "developmental" players (who have played in 140 or fewer games). WCHL attendance exceeded 1 million fans in a season for the first time in 1998.

Canadian Hockey League: This organization actually consists of 3 minor leagues in Canada and the Northwest United States – the Western Hockey League (19 teams in Western Canada and the Northwest U.S.), the Ontario Hockey League (20 teams in Ontario), and the Quebec Major Junior Hockey League (16 teams in Quebec, New Brunswick and Nova Scotia). These leagues provide much of the talent chosen in the annual NHL entry *draft*.

ROLLER HOCKEY LEAGUES
The growing worldwide popularity of inline skating over the past decade has fueled interest in the sport of roller

hockey as an alternative to ice hockey for recreational players both young and old. In this sport, players wear roller blades and play on a slick plastic surface called a "Sport Court" that allows a specially designed *puck* to move quickly across it. Today, participation in roller hockey has already exceeded that of ice hockey in the U.S. due to the wide availability of roller hockey rinks and the ease of playing the sport recreationally on just about any hard surface.

Professional leagues quickly sprung up to capitalize on this popularity, including *Roller Hockey International* (*RHI*) founded in 1993 and *Major League Roller Hockey* (*MLRH*) in 1997. However, they eventually encountered financial difficulties due to high operating expenses and the lack of a national television contract. The only league to survive was MLRH, which was re-launched in 2000 as an amateur league and has thrived on a more modest scale.

Major League Roller Hockey (MLRH): This amateur league consists of 14 teams in Colorado and the mid-Atlantic U.S., with plans to expand to about 20 teams in 2003. Each team plays a 12-game season that runs from January to May, culminating in a championship game played in Denver. Teams play 5 players per side (*4-on-4* plus a goalie) for four 12-minute quarters, and ties are decided first by a 5-minute sudden-death overtime period followed by a five-man shootout. Games are played with a black PRO-SHOT™ *puck* made by IDS (Ideal Design Sports) which is constructed of PVC plastic and rides on 8 polymer glide pins around its perimeter for maximum speed. Each team can carry a roster of up to 18 players who may be of any experience level.

TABLE OF CONTENTS

THE ORIGINS OF HOCKEY

No one is quite sure where hockey began. Several countries claim they invented the sport — the Irish game of hurley bears a close resemblance, while the French claim the name is derived from the French word "hoquet" (shepherd's crook). A similar game, hockie, was played in Galway as far back as 1527.

North American ice hockey most likely originated in Canada where it is rumored soldiers began to informally pass a ball around on the ice. In 1879, W.F. Robertson and R.F. Smith, two students at Montreal's McGill University, tried to adapt field hockey to ice and devised the first official rules and regulations. Not surprisingly, the first team to play by these prearranged rules was the McGill University Club during the 1880-81 season.

The Amateur Hockey Association of Canada was formed around 1889, and by the turn of the century there were many teams in assorted leagues. The National Hockey Association was formed in 1910; it was the forerunner of the *National Hockey League* (*NHL*) which was formed in 1917.

The game was first played with a wooden disk, which was later replaced with a more durable rubber lacrosse ball. This worked well outdoors, but in indoor games the bouncing ball broke windows. Today's flat *puck* was born when a frustrated *rink* owner, trying to prevent further damage, took a knife and sliced off the top and bottom of the ball. Many such equipment changes and rule changes have characterized the evolution of hockey since the NHL began.

THE OBJECT OF ICE HOCKEY

The simplest explanation of ice hockey is to say it is a fast-paced game played on a frozen ice surface by two teams of 6 players each. These players wear *skates* and carry a wooden *stick* that curves at the bottom. They use the sticks to push the playing piece, called a *puck*, across the ice and into a *net* to score *points*, which are called *goals*. The object of the game is for each team to try to score more goals than its opponent.

The principle guiding the rules of hockey is that of continuous action. Only the *officials* can stop the game and then only under certain circumstances. If a player has personal difficulties, such as a minor injury, wanting or needing a rest, having his shorts fall off while on the ice, or even breaking his stick, he must deal with these problems while the game continues.

Keeping this simple summary of the game in mind, you can now review each of the sections describing the rules, strategies and player positions to get a more complete view of ice hockey. Most of the rules are quite logical, stemming from a desire to keep the game moving while trying to protect players from serious injury. If you remember these two overall concerns in hockey, you will have little trouble understanding the rules of the game.

Ice hockey is an exciting game, and once you learn its relatively simple rules, you will be well on your way to enjoying this spectacular sport.

THE HOCKEY RINK

Ice hockey is played on an indoor ice surface called a *rink*, located inside an arena. (See **Figure 1**) Each professional team has its own arena located in its home city, and while there are some differences between the arenas (such as the seating capacity), the similarities are vast.

The rink size is 200 feet long by 85 feet wide with rounded corners. Wooden or fiberglass walls surround the rink to protect the fans and prevent the *puck* (and players) from accidentally leaving the area. These walls, called *boards*, are 3½ - 4 feet high; they are called *sideboards* along the length of the rink and *endboards* behind the *goals*. Today, rinks also have shatterproof glass that rises above the boards to provide even greater protection from flying pucks. In 2002, after a spectator died from injuries caused by a flying puck, the first such occurrence in NHL history, the league mandated that netting be added above the glass in the corners and ends of the rink, and that the glass extend at least 5 feet above the sideboards.

Lines are drawn on the ice and another layer of ice is frozen over them. These lines are continued and drawn up along the boards as well. The diagram on the next page might help you to picture these better.

- *Blue lines* divide the ice into three equal sections; these are called the *defending zone*, the *attacking zone* and the *neutral zone* in between them.

- A red *center line* divides the ice surface in half; it is located in the neutral zone, between the two blue lines.

- Two red *goal lines* are located 13 feet in from the endboards, one at each end of the rink. This distance was increased from 11 feet in 1998 to provide better scoring opportunities by giving *passers* more room to maneuver behind the *net*.

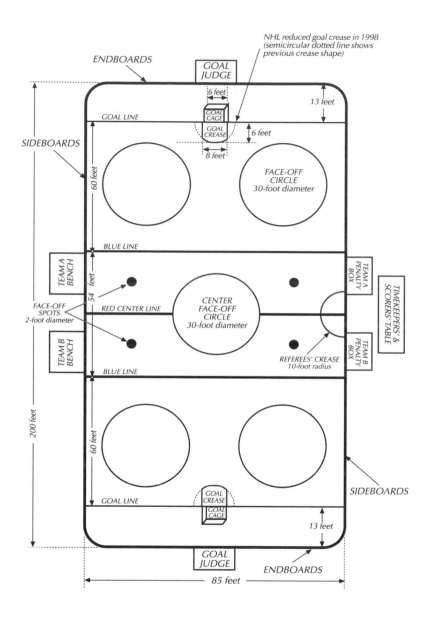

Figure 1: A hockey rink.

4

Centered on each red goal line is a *goal cage*. (See **Figure 2**) The goal cage consists of a tubular frame with two *goalposts* joined at the top by a metal *cross bar*, 4 feet high and 6 feet wide. It is through this opening that the puck must pass to score a *goal*, and one player stands in front of each goal to protect it; he is called the *goalie*. When a goal is scored, a red light located behind the goal is turned on to show that a team has scored a point. A *net*, made of white nylon cord, is draped over and attached to the frame to reduce the chance of the puck coming out or passing through without being detected as a goal; it extends back about 4 feet. This entire area is often referred to as

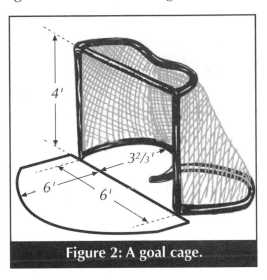

Figure 2: A goal cage.

the goal or the net. Drawn on the ice in front of the goal is the *goal crease*, a semi-circular area with a 6 foot radius. An attacking player positioned in this area may not make contact with the goalie or impede his movement or vision, or any goal scored will be disallowed. The size of the NHL's crease was reduced near the corners of the goal starting with the 1998-99 season to lower the number of goals disallowed because of crease infractions. Any player can skate in the area behind each net.

Each team's goalie stays near its goal to try and prevent the puck from being placed in it by the other team. The goalie and his goal are both said to be in his team's defending zone, which is the attacking zone for the other team. **An easy way to remember it is to think: Team A**

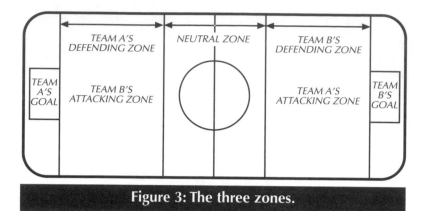

is trying to stop, or *defend*, the *attack* of Team B. Therefore, when we are in Team A's *defending* zone, we are also in Team B's *attacking* zone. At the opposite end of the ice is Team B's goal and Team B's defending zone which is also Team A's attacking zone. Here, Team B tries to stop, or defend, the attack of Team A. As you can see, one team's defending zone is always the other team's attacking zone. (See **Figure 3**)

There are also several circles and other lines drawn on the ice. The circles are used by the *referees* or *linesmen* to put the puck back into play and start the action again whenever it has stopped, through a procedure called a *face-off* which is discussed in the chapter on **HOW THE GAME IS PLAYED**. Altogether, there are 9 circles and 3 semi-circular areas drawn on the ice:

- The large blue circle in the middle of the rink is called the *center face-off circle.*

- There are four red *face-off spots* in the neutral zone.

- Two more red *face-off circles* are located at each end of the rink near the goal lines.

- Two semi-circular areas, one in front of each goal, are called the goal creases and denote the playing areas of each goalie, within which attacking players must avoid impeding the goalie or risk having any goal scored disallowed.

- A semi-circular area with a 10-foot radius in front of the *timekeepers' table* is the *referees' crease*, an area into which no player may follow the referee.

On one side of the rink, behind the sideboards, there are two team *benches*, one for each of the teams. Although only 6 players are on the ice at one time, there are usually 20 players on a team. These other players sit on the bench until it is time for them to *substitute* for players on the ice. Since they need to skate onto the ice quickly to substitute, these benches are located just off the ice. The coaches, managers and team trainers also sit on this bench throughout the game. The *timekeepers* and *official scorer* sit across the ice at a special table located between the two *penalty boxes*.

A penalty box is where players are sent to sit for a specified period of time after they have broken a rule (committed a *penalty*). A player will sit on a bench in the penalty box until his penalty time is up (expires), and then he will rejoin his team.

Now let us see what **UNIFORMS & EQUIPMENT** players use.

UNIFORMS & EQUIPMENT

Professional hockey players wear special uniforms and ice skates with boots. Each player carries a stick to move the puck. (See **Figure** 4) Goalies use different equipment from the rest of the players.

STICKS

Hockey players use L-shaped wooden, aluminum, graphite or fiberglass *sticks* which are viewed as two connected parts: the handle, or shaft, curves around into the bottom part called the blade. The area where the shaft and blade meet is called the heel. Sticks can be a maximum of 63 inches long measured from the heel to the end of the shaft. The blade must not exceed 12 $\frac{1}{2}$ inches in length, must be between 2 and 3 inches in height, and must have beveled edges. The blade can have a very slight curve (limited to $\frac{1}{2}$ inch) and can be angled to the left or the right. Most hockey players go through several sticks a season and have sticks that suit their particular style of playing. Adhesive tape may be wrapped around the stick at any place for the purpose of reinforcement or to improve the handling of the stick; use of tape will also vary with individual players.

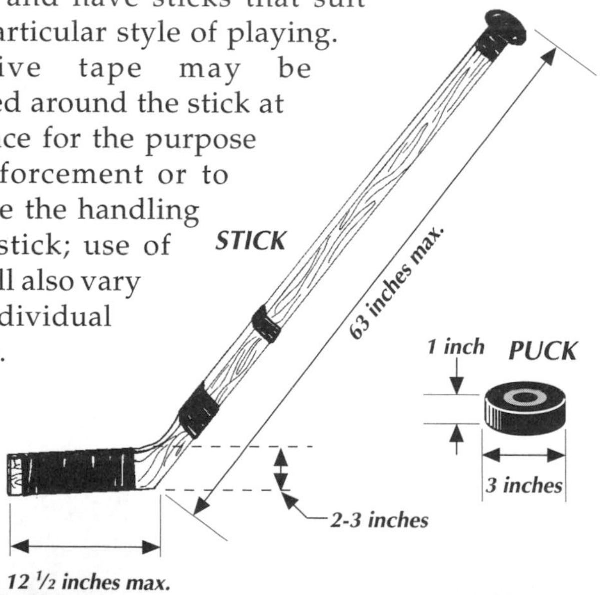

STICK

63 inches max.

1 inch   PUCK

3 inches

2-3 inches

12 $\frac{1}{2}$ inches max.

Figure 4: Stick and puck.

Goalies carry slightly different sticks than the other players: the shaft must have a knob of adhesive tape at least ½ an inch thick at the top and the blade measures no more than 15 ½ by 3 ½ inches. Unlike other players who can skate to their *bench* to replace a broken stick, the goalie must wait for a teammate to bring him a new stick from the bench or else he incurs a *penalty*.

PUCK

Hockey is played with a vulcanized hard rubber disk called a *puck*, 1 inch thick and 3 inches in diameter, weighing between 5 ½ and 6 ounces. To reduce the bounce of the rubber and to increase their speed to over 100 miles per hour, pucks are frozen before each game and changed throughout the game.

SKATES AND BOOTS

Each player wears special ice hockey skates with sharp steel blades that are *rockered*, or curved up at the front and back. (See **Figure 5**) Rockered blades make it easier for players to start and turn quickly. Blades are sharpened for each game. For protection,

Figure 5: Skates and boots.

boots are strong and heavily padded around the ankle. The boots of goalies and *defensemen* are stronger than those of the *forwards*. It is not unusual for a professional player to wear out or break several pairs of skates each season.

NON-GOALIE EQUIPMENT & UNIFORMS

Defensemen and forwards wear the same basic protective padded clothing and uniform. (See **Figure 6**) They start with special perspiration-absorbing underwear and long footless stockings which cover hard plastic padded shin guards. Under a loose-fitting team jersey and knee-length nylon shorts held up by suspenders or a built-in belt, they wear shoulder pads with rib protection attached, elbow pads, and an athletic supporter with protective cup. Their shorts act as a girdle and have built-in pads to protect their hips, thighs and the area near their kidneys. Defensemen may add ankle guards to prevent bruising or breakage. All the players wear padded *gloves* with cuffs that slightly overlap the elbow pads to protect the forearm. These gloves cannot have holes in them that would allow fingers to protrude and be used to hold onto or grab an opponent's uniform.

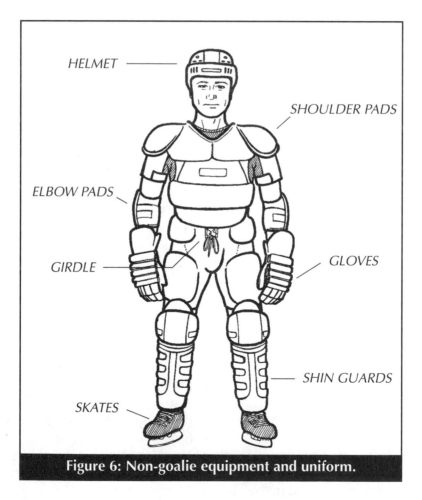

Figure 6: Non-goalie equipment and uniform.

The team jersey is generally white for the home team and dark for the visiting team. This makes it easier to distinguish teams. On the front of the jersey is the team logo and on the back is the player's name and number. When a player is the team *captain*, a three-inch C is on the front; a three-inch A denotes the alternate captain(s).

HEAD GEAR

Players were not always required to wear a *helmet*. Today, helmets are mandatory equipment for all NHL players, although as recently as 1997, certain veteran players who had never played with one were exempted from the rule. The helmet is a light weight, plastic-padded head protector with ventilation holes and slots so that the player's head does not get too warm. The goalie wears a hard helmet as well as a mask that covers his face.

GOALIE UNIFORMS

Goalies start with the same basic uniform as their teammates, but they wear additional protective equipment weighing an extra 20 pounds or more. Instead of shin guards they wear large pads, up to 12 inches wide and 3-4 inches thick, around each leg from the ankle to the thighs, and they also wear thicker pads on their shoulders, arms and chest. The padding protecting their crotch is also thicker than that of their teammates. A goalie uses two different kinds of gloves, one for each hand. The glove for the hand that holds his stick is made of padded leather or leather-like plastic and has a large rectangular pad attached to the front of it. Called the blocking glove or *waffle pad*, it is used to deflect the puck when it is shot at his goal. On the other hand he wears a catching glove, with which he can catch or scoop up the puck and hold it or drop it away from the goal. Even goalies' skates are different; they are heavier than those of their teammates and there is almost no open space between the skate blade and the bottom of the boot to prevent the puck from accidentally passing through the skate and into the goal.

ZAMBONI

The machine used to "flood" the ice, or clean it and smooth it out, is called a *Zamboni*, named after its inventor, Frank Zamboni. Two Zambonis make an appearance before the start of every *period*, taking about 10 minutes to clean the ice.

EQUIPMENT VIOLATIONS

A goalie may not wear extra equipment, and players are not permitted to wear anything the officials consider dangerous to himself or to other players. No non-goalie player is allowed to wear a mask (unless he has a facial injury). Whenever a team believes a player on the other team is playing with equipment that is not regulation dimensions (for example a blade with too much curvature), a formal complaint can be made to the *referee* by the captain or alternate captain. The referee will take the suspicious equipment to the *timekeeper*, who will make the necessary measurement and report it to the *penalty timekeeper* who records it. If the complaint is justified, the player committing the infraction is assessed a *minor penalty* and fined. If it is not, the team that requested the measurement is penalized.

Now let us see **HOW THE GAME IS PLAYED**.

HOW THE GAME IS PLAYED

Five of the 6 players on each team skate around the ice trying to put the playing piece, called a *puck*, into the *net* to score *points*, called *goals*. The team that has the most goals at the end of the game is the winner.

LENGTH OF THE GAME
In the *NHL*, each game has three 20-minute *periods* with a 15-minute *intermission* between each period. A large clock counts down the minutes and seconds of playing time to show the players and fans how much time is left in each period. The clock is stopped when the playing stops, and started up again when the playing resumes. Each professional hockey game has 3 periods of play and 2 intermissions (called a *regulation* game) which take 90 minutes. However, a game always takes much longer than 90 minutes to complete, usually 2 to 3 hours, due to stoppages of play. Players take a warm-up before each period begins by skating around their end of the rink. Also before the start of each period you will see the *Zambonis* cleaning the ice and smoothing it out to prepare it for play.

OVERTIME
One *sudden-death overtime* period of 5 minutes is played if both teams are *tied* at the end of regulation during *regular-season* games. It begins after the third period ends following a two-minute rest period. To make the extra period more exciting and increase the chances of a tie-breaking goal, the NHL adopted a new rule in 1999 that reduces the number of overtime *skaters* per team from 5 to 4 (called *4-on-4*), except during the playoffs. Sudden-death means the first team to score a goal wins and the game ends, even if the overtime period is not completed. If both teams are still tied after one overtime period, the game ends in a tie score. The exception to this is during the *post-season* (or *playoffs*) where there can be no tied games. After a 15-minute intermission, play continues

into as many 20-minute overtime periods as are needed to determine a winner.

TIME-OUTS
Each team is permitted only one 30-second *time-out* per game which can only be taken when play has already stopped. Otherwise, only the *referee* can stop play, even if a player is seriously *injured*. "Official time-outs" are frequently called to allow broadcasters to insert commercials throughout the game and are not charged to either team.

ATTACKING: TRYING TO SCORE GOALS
Skaters skate at about 20 miles per hour and move the puck with their sticks. When a player's stick is touching the puck and moving it, he is "in control of the puck" (he is called the *puck carrier*) and it is said that his team "has the puck", or is in *possession* of the puck. He can maneuver the puck and attempt to score a goal; therefore his team is called the attacking team, or *offense*.

The player with the puck has several options: he can try to *shoot* the puck for a goal if he is close enough to the net and sees a good opportunity, or he can *pass* the puck to one of his teammates.

It is legal for a player to *kick* the puck, except to score a goal. Such goals will be disallowed. Kicking is an acceptable and proper tactic for a player who has lost his stick or even if he has a stick but cannot get into position fast enough to play the puck with it. A player may also direct a puck with his open hand so that he may play it

Figure 7: Slap shot.

14

with his stick. He can also catch it and drop it. However, he may not direct it with his hands into the goal or to a teammate, except from his *defending zone*.

Shooting

A player shoots the puck towards an opponent's goal in an attempt to score. A player can take several different kinds of shots, depending on the situation, by propelling the puck with his stick in one of these ways:

- *Slap shot*: (See **Figure 7**) achieves an extremely high speed but is less accurate than a *wrist shot*; player raises his stick in a backswing, with his strong hand held low on the shaft and his other hand on the end as a pivot; as the stick comes down towards the puck, the player leans into the stick to put all his power behind the shot, adding velocity to the puck.

- *Wrist shot*: made with the stick blade kept on the ice; the hockey puck is propelled across the ice and towards the net by a strong flicking of the wrists; slower but usually more accurate than a slap shot.

- *Backhand shot*: like the wrist shot except the shot is taken from the backhand rather than forehand.

- *Flip shot*: the puck is cupped in the stick blade, then flipped with the wrists off the ice up towards the goal.

Passing

Passing is when one player uses his stick to send the puck to a teammate. Passing is used to move the puck closer to the goal, to keep the puck away from the opponents or to give the puck to the player that is in the best position to score. There are several different types of passes that players use:

- *Flat pass*: a player passes the puck to a teammate along the surface of the ice.

- *Flip pass*: a player passes the puck to a teammate by lifting it with his stick into the air.

- *Drop pass*: a player simply leaves the puck behind for a teammate to pick up.

When a pass is to be sent to a teammate that is moving, the passer needs to "lead" his teammate with a *lead pass*. This means the passer will send the puck to where he expects the moving player to be when the pass arrives.

DEFENSE: STOPPING THE TEAM WITH THE PUCK FROM SCORING

During a hockey game, possession of the puck constantly changes back and forth between opposing teams. The team without the puck at any moment during the game is considered the *defense* or defending team. Its mission is to try and get the puck away from the other team and prevent it from scoring. One of the 6 players from each team is allowed to stand in front of the goal to protect it and prevent shots from going in for a score. This player is called the *goalie* and more information on him and his teammates is in the chapter on **THE TEAM & PLAYER POSITIONS**.

The other 5 players on the defending team skate around and try to intercept the puck as it is being passed, block shots headed towards the goal, or take the puck away from a player that has it on his stick. The two legal, permissible methods for stopping an opponent are *checking* and *blocking*:

- Checking: bumping into an opponent by using the stick, shoulders or hips. (See **Figure 8**) Checking is only allowed against the player in control of the puck or against the last player to control it immediately after he gives it up. There are two main types of checks: *stick checks* and *body checks*. In a stick check, a player uses his stick to hook, poke or sweep the puck away from an opponent. In a body check a player bumps or slams into an opponent with either his hip

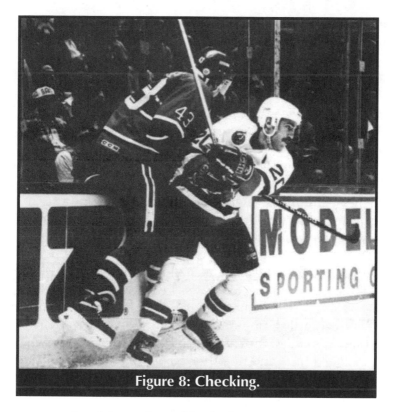

Figure 8: Checking.

or shoulder <u>only</u> to block the opponent's progress or throw him off-balance.

- Blocking: a less common method where a player drops to one or both knees and uses his body to stop a puck; this is riskier because a smart puck carrier may be able to get around a defender that drops to his knees too soon.

Since skaters move pretty fast, there are many hard checks and physical plays. However, the players are well protected by their equipment which was described more fully in the chapter on **UNIFORMS & EQUIPMENT**.

It is when a player uses other, illegal methods to get the puck or stop his opponents that the referee will call a penalty. Penalties are discussed in great detail in the chapter entitled

PENALTIES, and reading about them will help you recognize when an infraction occurs.

CHOOSING SIDES FOR THE GAME
The home team starts the game defending the goal closest to its team *bench*. The teams then switch the goals they defend each successive period, including overtime periods in the playoffs.

STARTING PLAY: FACE-OFFS
At the beginning of each period, and to start play after it has been stopped during the game, a *face-off* (also known as the *draw* or the *drop*) is used. (See **Figure 9**) A face-off is a fair way to ensure that both teams have an equal chance of gaining access to the puck, although some players are better than others at winning face-offs. In a face-off an *official* drops the puck on the ice between the sticks of two opposing players standing one stick-length apart, each facing his opponent's end of the ice. The blades of their sticks must be touching the ice, and no other player may be within 15 feet of them. These two opposing players compete to touch the puck first and direct it to one of their teammates. If either of

Figure 9: Face-off.

these players is not in the proper position when the official is ready to drop the puck, the official may order a teammate of that player to take the face-off instead. This is why you may see a player who is set up for a face-off skate off unexpectedly to be replaced by a teammate in the *face-off circle*. A new NHL procedure introduced in 2002 to speed up games dictates that the puck be dropped within 20 seconds of a stoppage (except during the final 2 minutes of a game or in overtime), whether or not both players have established their positions at the *face-off spot* or circle.

The face-off spots and circles are located at various places around the rink. Generally, unless the rules specify otherwise, a face-off is held near the place where the infraction occurred or where play was stopped. One exception is if the stoppage has been caused by an attacking player in his *attacking zone*, then the resulting face-off is taken back in the *neutral zone*.

STOPPING PLAY
There are several reasons why play may be stopped during the period:

- if a player breaks a rule and receives a penalty
- if the goalie stops a shot and holds onto the puck
- if the puck goes "out of play" or flies out of the rink
- if the referee determines a player is seriously injured
- if the *goal cage* is dislodged and moves off its spot
- if a player is injured and his team has possession of the puck
- if a player catches the puck in his hand and it is declared *dead*
- if the referee loses sight of the puck in a crowd of players
- if the puck cannot be moved after being stuck underneath a player or between a player's stick or skate and the *boards*; the puck is said to be *frozen*

A GAME OF CONSTANT MOTION
In general, the puck must always be kept in motion. The team in possession of the puck can carry it behind its own goal only once and must advance it towards the opposing goal unless prevented from doing so by opposing players. A player who deliberately freezes the puck, falls on it, holds it, or plays it along the boards in such a way to stop play will be assessed a penalty unless he is being checked by an opponent. A player outside his defensive zone may not pass or carry the puck back into his own zone in order to stall for time, unless his team has fewer players on the ice than the opposition (called being *shorthanded*).

Formal plays in hockey are not as common as in other sports because possession of the puck is fleeting. The speed and contact allowed by the rules make it difficult for players to complete plays requiring precise timing. Therefore, rather than established plays, in ice hockey play generally follows the puck, which moves quickly all over the rink, and players must improvise actions to score.

END OF GAME SPORTSMANSHIP
At the end of every game, all the hockey players of both teams line up at opposite sides of the rink and skate toward each other so that each player on one team can shake hands with each player on the opposing team. This tradition is unique among professional sports and reminds players of the importance of good sportsmanship.

The next few sections should help you to identify the different players, reasons why play has stopped and the rule violations that the officials are looking for.

THE TEAM & PLAYER POSITIONS

Each hockey team may have a maximum of 6 players on the ice at one time. The first 6 players to begin the game for a team are called the *starting lineup*. Each player has a certain job to do, and plays a certain position. The 6 positions generally played are *goalkeeper* (or *goalie*), *left defenseman, right defenseman, center, left wing* and *right wing*. The goalie stays near his team's goal; of the 5 players that skate around the rink (called *skaters*), the left and right defensemen comprise the team's *defensive line*, and the center, left and right wing together make up the *forward line*. (See **Figure 10**)

Today, 20 players, including 2 goalkeepers, are a standard complete *NHL* team. A team usually will have 3 forward

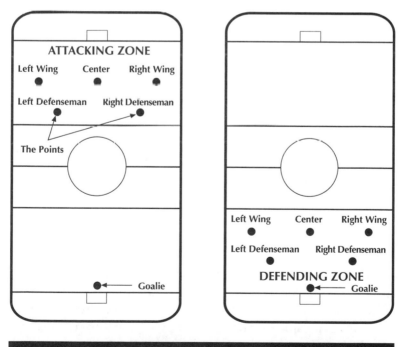

Figure 10: Player positions.

21

lines (9 players) and 5 or 6 defensemen to rotate in; the other 3 or 4 players are usually spare forwards or *penalty killers*.

SHORTHANDED / POWER PLAYS

When a player commits a *penalty*, his team may have to play with one less player than the other team, or *shorthanded*. The other team, which now has the advantage of outnumbering the shorthanded team, is said to be on the *power play*. These concepts are discussed further in the chapter on **PENALTIES**.

SUBSTITUTIONS

Substitutions may be made at any time during play stoppages or while play is in progress, provided a team at no time has more than 6 players on the ice. Most often, substitutions are made *on-the-fly*, with substitutes skating into the game and players leaving the ice as play continues around them. The moment the player leaving the ice gets within 5 feet of the *bench*, his substitute can go over the *boards* and come into play. This type of substitution is why you may occasionally see a player skate right by the *puck* at the *sideboards*; if a substituting player touches the puck before the retiring player has completely left the ice, their team could be penalized for having *too many men on the ice*.

Some *coaches* change everyone except the goalie every 2-3 minutes to provide adequate rest. A goalie will usually play the entire game unless he gets injured or is playing very poorly. Unlike other sports where individuals are substituted for individuals, in hockey the entire forward line often will be replaced at once, putting players on the ice who work well together. This is called a *line change*. Scoring goals often requires precision and timing which is achieved by practice and familiarity among teammates. Also, when a *referee* stops play because he believes a player is seriously injured, that player must be substituted for immediately, unless he is the goalie.

THE FORWARD LINE
The forward line plays nearer to the opponent's *goal* and is responsible for most of the scoring. It is comprised of three players: the right and left wings and a center.

Center
The center usually leads his team's attack when it is trying to score a *goal*. He also takes part in most of the *face-offs*. The center must be able to think and react quickly. He starts play in the center of the forward line, but the playing action can take him anywhere on the ice as he pursues the puck. Since he often possesses the puck as he and his teammates are skating toward the other team's goal, he must be able to control the puck while he is moving and be able to pass it to a teammate who is in a position to take a shot towards the goal. Good centers score many *goals* and usually have even more *assists* (as discussed in the chapter on **TEAM & INDIVIDUAL SCORING**).

Left and Right Wing
Each wing skates along the left or right side of the *rink* on either side of the center, approaching the goal from an angle which gives him more openings to shoot at the goal. Wings pass the puck to each other and to the center, trying to get the puck to the player who has the best shot at the goal. Good wings usually score more goals and dole out fewer assists than centers. Although left and right wings cover their respective left and right sides, like the center, they can be found anywhere on the ice.

DEFENSEMEN
The *left* and *right defensemen* generally play to the rear of the team so they are available to defend their own goal. The left defenseman covers the left half of the rink and the right defenseman plays to the right, harassing the right and left wings on the other team, but they can skate into each other's territory.

Defensemen actually have a two-part job:

- When their team is defending (the opponents have the puck) the defensemen will use *checking* and *blocking* to try to steal the puck or make it impossible for the opponents to continue their attack. In the defending situation, once the puck has crossed the *blue line* into the *defending zone*, usually you will see one defenseman station himself near the goal to assist his goalie, while the other defenseman goes after the player controlling the puck.

- When their team is on the attack (has the puck), they try to keep the puck in their *attacking zone* by passing it to their teammates. They position themselves on opposite sides of the ice just inside the blue line at locations called the *points* (see **Figure 10** on page 21). When playing there, the defensemen themselves are also called points or "point men". If the defending team mounts a sudden counter-attack, they use *backchecking* (*checking* while skating back towards their own goal) to break it up.

Defensemen are highly skilled at skating backwards, checking (moving their bodies against the person with the puck and making them lose control of the puck) and blocking shots at the goal. They are often the biggest, strongest members of the team. Sometimes defensemen can even lead an attack and score; a few of the NHL's top scorers have been defensemen.

GOALKEEPER
He is also called the goalie, goaltender or netminder. (See **Figure 11**) The goalie generally plays the entire game unless he is injured or plays very poorly. He does not skate around the ice like his teammates; his job is to stay near his team's goal and protect it. His area is the *goal crease* in front of the goal.

Figure 11: Goalkeeper.

In playing position, the goalie's feet are just wide enough apart so that his heavy leg pads are close together, with his knees slightly bent and flexible to allow him to move in either direction quickly. His body is bent forward at the waist so he can watch the puck, and he holds his *stick* flat on the ice in front of his skates with one hand. The other hand with the catching *glove* is ready to grab or bat at a flying puck.

The rules of hockey give the goalie certain privileges that other players do not have. He is the only player who can pick up and handle the puck or *freeze* it with his hands or body, although he may do so only when in his goal crease and pressured by opposing players. Also, opposing players may not make deliberate contact with the goalie either inside or outside his goal crease, nor may they obstruct his movement or vision while within the crease. Any goal scored in these cases will be disallowed.

The goalie tries to stop the puck (which may be traveling up to 120 miles per hour) any way he can. A shot by an attacking player that would become a goal if not *saved* by the goalie is called a *shot on goal*. One of the NHL's early rules made it a $2 fine for a goalie to lie down on the ice to block a shot on goal. Today a goalie can use virtually any means available to him to stop a shot. In addition to lying flat, he can block the shot with his gloves or his heavily padded arms and legs, he can use his stick to block or bat away a shot, or he can scoop up the puck with his special catching glove and drop it away from the goal. However, it is often wise for a goalie who is surrounded by attackers to hold onto the puck after he stops it to prevent giving the attacking team a second chance to score. Popular styles of goaltending include *butterfly style, standup style* and *hybrid style*.

Many people think the goalie has the hardest job of all because he alone must keep the other team from scoring until his teammates are able to regain control of the puck. The goalie must have extremely fast reflexes and must be alert to the progress of the game. He and his teammates have to ensure that he can see the puck at all times, or his opponents may be able to sneak a shot past him and into the net.

PENALTY KILLERS
Certain players on a team are expert at backchecking and keeping or gaining control of a loose puck under difficult circumstances. The coach will send them in when the team is shorthanded to defend against power plays until the players in the *penalty box* serve their time and return to the game. These terms are discussed more fully in the chapter entitled **PENALTIES**.

ENFORCERS
A team may have a *policeman* or *enforcer*. He is usually the most penalized player on a team because his job is to protect his teammates from harm. The enforcer is usually a larger player who is not afraid to fight or otherwise stand up to his opponents.

26

TEAM & INDIVIDUAL SCORING

The object of hockey is for one team to score more *goals* than the other to win the game. A legal goal is scored when the *puck* goes between the *goalposts* off the *stick* of an attacking player and crosses completely over the red *goal line*. A goal is not scored if the puck bounces off an *official*. The puck may not be kicked, thrown, batted by hand or deliberately directed into the net by any means other than the stick of an attacking player held below the level of the goal *cross bar*. It is a legal score, however, if a defender accidentally bumps the puck in or if it has been deflected off of any player into the goal. When the puck deflects off of an attacking player into the goal, that player is credited with the goal.

The *referee* can disallow a goal if, in his judgment at the time of the goal, a player on the attacking team positioned inside the *goal crease* impaired the ability of the *goalie* to defend his goal by impeding his movement, initiating contact with him or obstructing his vision. The goal should not be disallowed if the attacker in the crease was pushed there by a defending opponent. The referee's decision cannot be assisted by *video replay*. This "no harm, no foul, no video review" rule was first instituted for the 1999-2000 season, replacing an old rule that disqualified any goal that occurred while an attacking player was positioned in the crease, regardless of whether or not his presence impacted the goalie.

When a player passes the puck to a teammate who scores, it is said he has provided assistance, or an *assist*, to the goal scorer. It is even possible for two players to pass the puck, one immediately after the other, to a third player who then scores a goal. In such a case, both players may be credited with an assist. Giving credit for assists is not as clear cut as goal scoring; it is at the discretion of the *official scorer* to decide, and he is encouraged to use video replay to verify his decision.

When a goal is scored, the referee reports it to the official scorer. A few seconds later, the public will hear an announcement similar to this: "Goal scored for the Flyers, by number 10, *John LeClair*, with assists from number 8, Mark Recchi and number 97, Jeremy Roenick." As this example shows, assists can be credited to two players for each one goal scored, but it is not mandatory. In sum, a player can score a goal unassisted, or with the assist of one or two players.

In addition to affecting the final game score, goals and assists play a role in each player's individual scoring record. In the individual records, an assist and a goal each are worth one *point*. At the end of a season, a player will have accumulated a certain number of points, which is his total number of goals added to his total number of assists:

GOALS + ASSISTS = POINTS

A *hat trick* is where a player scores 3 or more goals in a single game, truly an accomplishment.

A list of the career and single-season scoring leaders is in the chapter on **NHL INDIVIDUAL RECORDS**.

THE OFFICIALS

The general conduct of a hockey game is under the charge of two *referees* assisted by two *linesmen* on the ice who call infractions and hand out *penalties*. The *NHL* increased the number of referees from one to two in all games starting with the 2000-01 season. There are also off-ice *officials* including two *goal judges*, a *game timekeeper*, a *penalty timekeeper*, an *official scorer*, a *statistician* with assistants and a *video goal judge*. To communicate, the on-ice officials use *hand signals* and phrases that the other officials are able to interpret to keep accurate records and convey the on-ice decisions to the fans. The hand signals for the most commonly called infractions are provided in the chapter called **OFFICIALS' HAND SIGNALS**. Once an official signals a penalty, he reports the uniform number(s) of the guilty player(s) to be announced twice over the public address system. Keep in mind that if a *puck* strikes an official, play will continue uninterrupted because in hockey, an official is considered part of the *rink*, much like the *boards* or *goalposts*.

REFEREES

The men on skates wearing black pants and official league sweaters with orange armbands are in charge and responsible for the orderly progress of the game. They each carry a whistle, a tape measure, and a stick-measuring gauge. In general, the referees are responsible for starting the game, making sure the ice, *nets* and clock are in good condition, seeing that the other officials are present and ready for the game, and imposing penalties. Each has the power to send a player to the *penalty box* and can decide that a player is *injured* seriously enough to stop play. They can retreat into an area called the *referees' crease*, located in front of the *timekeepers' table* in the rink, and no player may follow them into this area without permission or a *misconduct penalty* will be called. The referees report *goals* to the scorers' table so their decision can be announced to the fans. They must be able to see the puck at all times, or they will stop play and hold a *face-off*.

LINESMEN

Two other men on skates, one positioned toward each end of the rink, assist the referees. They wear black pants and an official league sweater (but without red armbands) and also carry whistles, tape measures and stick-measuring gauges. These linesmen call *offsides*, *icing*, and most play stoppages and handle most face-offs. They are also responsible for breaking up any fights, allowing the referees to watch the action and decide which penalties to call. Linesmen call *minor penalties* that they observe in addition to drawing the referees' attention to any goal or infraction they may not have seen. The linesmen also retrieve the puck when play is stopped.

GOAL JUDGES

One person behind each goal decides when a puck has crossed the goal line and will switch on a red light to signal that a goal has been scored. They are stationed in two separate protected areas behind the opposite *endboards*, positioned so they can easily see the play and puck near the goals. Their decisions are simple: either a goal has been scored or not. The referee can overrule the goal judge's decision and disallow a goal.

GAME TIMEKEEPER

One person controls the official timing device during the three 20-minute *periods* and any *overtime* that is played. The game timekeeper watches the master clock and signals the end of each period, records the time at which the game and each of the periods starts and ends, stops the clock every time the whistle blows, starts it again when the puck is dropped in a face-off, sounds the device which indicates the end of the period and instructs the public-address announcer to inform all present when there is only one minute left to play in a period.

PENALTY TIMEKEEPER

Another timekeeper assists the game timekeeper by keeping track of every player sent to the penalty box and their respective sentences to ensure offenders serve the required time for their penalties. The penalty timekeeper keeps records of all penalties, of time served, and of any *penalty shots* taken on the ice, including the names of the shooters and the results of the shots.

OFFICIAL SCORER
The official scorer maintains a written record on a special form of the eligible players and *starting lineup* for each team, the number of goals, the player scoring each goal, the player(s) credited with an *assist*, the time at which each goal was scored, the total number of shots, the number of *saves* by each *goalie* and the penalties. Although it is a referee who designates the player to be credited with a goal, it is the scorer who decides who to credit with the assists. As such, he is located in a place where he has full view of the rink, and he also communicates with the public-address announcer who announces his decisions to the fans.

STATISTICIAN
One individual, with as many assistants as are needed, must correctly record for the official NHL records all the actions of all of the other officials, the players and both teams. Once a referee signs these records they become official, and copies are sent to each team and to the league office after each game.

VIDEO GOAL JUDGE
Certain situations involving the puck in and around the goal area and the clock are subject to review by a *video goal judge*. Reviews can be initiated either by a referee or the video goal judge himself and are limited to deciding whether the puck actually crossed the goal line, how it was directed into the goal, how much time remained on the clock when a goal was scored, and whether or not the net was dislodged before the score. The video goal judge can also be consulted by the referees to help determine which players should be credited with goals and assists.

PENALTIES

In hockey there are *team penalties* and *individual penalties* called by the *officials* when a player or players break rules. A team penalty generally results in a *face-off*. There are 6 categories of individual penalties: *minor, major, bench minor, match* (game), *misconduct* and the *penalty shot*, each of which is treated differently. A player who commits an individual infraction spends actual game time off the ice. His jersey number is displayed on the scoreboard next to the time remaining on his penalty.

Only a *captain* or alternate captain can question or discuss with a *referee* anything concerning the rules, and only when invited to do so by the referee; any other player who does so will be penalized. No player, including the captain, may protest a call or he will receive a minor penalty, and if he persists, a misconduct penalty and then a *game misconduct* will be added. The rules simply do not permit any players to complain about penalties.

Player actions meant to intentionally cause serious harm are also punishable by multiple-game suspensions and monetary fines imposed by the *NHL*. Such fines and suspensions are not discussed in great detail here, but can make for interesting news when they occur.

TEAM PENALTIES
These are the most common violations and they result only in a face-off.

Offsides
The purpose of the *offside* rule is to prevent an attacking player from waiting in front of the opponent's goal for a long pass from a teammate, giving him an easier chance to score. To prevent this, the rule requires that the attacking players must all follow the puck into the *attacking zone*; they may not go in ahead of the puck. (Exception: a player in control of the puck who enters the zone ahead of it.) An

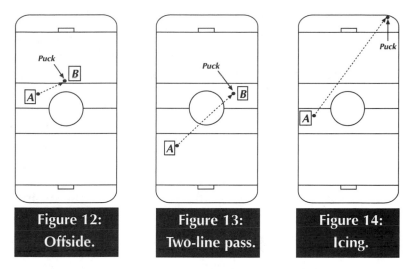

| Figure 12: Offside. | Figure 13: Two-line pass. | Figure 14: Icing. |

attacking player is considered offside if <u>both</u> his skates go over the *blue line* into the attacking zone before the puck does. (See **Figure 12**) If only one skate is over the blue line, with the player straddling the line, he is *onside* and there is no infraction. That is why you may sometimes see players skating strangely near the blue line. A face-off is held outside the attacking zone near the spot where the offside violation occurred.

An official may call a *delayed offside* by raising his arm but not blowing his whistle until he sees the outcome of the play (*slow whistle*). He may wait to call the penalty because if the defense is able to quickly get control of the puck, stopping the play would penalize the non-offending team by stopping its momentum. In this case, the offside is waved off, or cancelled, by the official and play continues uninterrupted.

Two-line Pass

The *two-line pass* (also known as an *offside pass*) is another type of offside violation. It occurs when a player passes the puck from his *defending zone* to a teammate across the red *center line*. (See **Figure 13**) However, like regular offsides it is no penalty if the puck precedes the player across the center line. A face-off is held at the point from which the illegal pass was made.

Icing

The *icing* infraction occurs when the team in possession of the puck shoots toward the goal from behind the red center line, the puck goes into the end of the rink across the red *goal line* (but not into the goal) and then a member of the opposing team other than the *goalie* touches the puck first. (See **Figure 14**) A face-off is then held in the penalized team's defending zone. It is not icing if the puck happens to go in the goal or if a member of the attacking team is the first to touch it. Icing is never called against a team that is playing *shorthanded* or if the puck is touched by the goalie or any other defender before it crosses the goal line. Additionally, an official who determines that a defender could have easily touched the puck before it crossed the goal line will not call icing.

Icing sometimes may be a good strategy for a team's players. It may provide them a break in the action, allowing for rest and substitutions, or may give them a chance to plan or change tactics, especially when the opponents are in a good position to score.

Other Penalties

The referee may stop play and call a face-off for certain infractions he deems unintentional and not directed against another player. Two such plays are batting a puck above the shoulders to a teammate with a *high stick* or briefly *carrying the puck* with the hand. Any non-goalie player is allowed to knock the puck down with his glove, but he can only slap or push it deliberately to a teammate if he is in his *defending zone*. If he does so outside his defending zone, it is called a *hand pass* violation and results in a face-off. Intentional infractions of these rules are discussed below under Individual Penalties.

INDIVIDUAL PENALTIES

Violations of certain rules punish the offending player by removing him from the action of the game and requiring him to serve actual playing time sitting on the *penalty bench* in the *penalty box* while his team plays with one less man. The penalized team will play with one less player than the other team, or *shorthanded*, unless the other team also has a player removed by a penalty, in which case the teams play at equal strength (neither is shorthanded). Most individual penalties are called because a player illegally interfered with an opponent, deliberately tried to hurt another player or played in a dangerous manner. Whenever a penalty is called, play stops, the penalized player leaves the ice and a face-off is used to restart the action. This face-off is usually held near the location where the infraction occurred, except when the violation was by a player in his attacking zone. In this case, the face-off is held at the nearest face-off spot in the neutral zone.

A team may also have to play with only 4 players (2 men short) if a second penalty is called against a player on the same team before the penalty against the first player expires. There is no limit to the number of penalties that can be called against a team. However, no matter how many penalties are called against a team, that team never plays with less than 4 men on the ice at a time (including one goalie).

Penalties that would cause a team to play with less than 4 men become *delayed penalties* and are served only as the time on prior penalties expires. Delayed penalties are then served in the order they were committed. When a third player is penalized after two of his teammates are already in the penalty box, he joins them in the penalty box but a substitute goes out to replace the third player on the ice. This substitution allows the team to keep playing with 4 players, but when the first penalized player's penalty time expires, he must go directly to the bench instead of back onto the ice. He can then only re-enter as a substitute.

The 6 types of individual rule violations and the penalty imposed for each are discussed on the following pages. Goalie penalties are treated separately. Each type of infraction is punishable by a specific length of time served in the penalty box. Sometimes multiple penalty types are imposed on a player in combination to suit the infraction, such as a major penalty plus a misconduct penalty. Note that any penalty time remaining at the end of a period will carry over and be served at the start of the next period.

The Power Play vs. Playing Shorthanded
When a team plays with all 6 players on the ice including the goalie, it is at *full strength*. When a team has fewer players on the ice than its opponent due to penalties, this is called playing shorthanded. When one team plays shorthanded, the other team enjoys a *power play*, one of the few set plays in hockey and one of the most exciting. In a power play, the team with more players on the ice tries to position all its players (except the goalie) in its attacking zone to take shot after shot at the goal, trying to overwhelm the opponent's goalie. The shorthanded team tries to *kill the penalty* (prevent their opponent from scoring until they are back at full strength). To respond to the power play, the shorthanded team often sends in substitute players called *penalty killers* who are expert at getting the puck away from the opponents, keeping it away by excellent stick handling and helping the goalie defend the goal.

Minor Penalties
A player who commits a minor infraction will spend 2 minutes in the penalty box. If his opponents score while he is in the penalty box and his team is shorthanded, the penalized player may return to the ice immediately. It used to be that a team stayed shorthanded the full 2 minutes of a minor penalty, but the *Montreal Canadiens* of the 1950s were so strong on the power play that they could score 2, 3 or as many as 4 goals during the 2 minutes. The rule used in the NHL today, where a penalized player returns to the ice as soon as <u>one goal</u> is scored, was changed to prevent such unbalanced scoring.

The most common minor penalties are those which endanger an opponent or impede his progress; less common are those called for equipment violations. The category of offenses includes *interference, tripping, boarding, cross-checking, slashing, charging, elbowing, holding, high-sticking, hooking,* closing the hand on the puck, playing with a broken stick, deliberately *falling on the puck,* holding the puck against the boards when not being checked, *leaving the bench illegally* and *roughing.* A rule even imposes a penalty on any player who fakes an action or takes a *dive* trying to draw a penalty call on the opposing team. When a minor penalty is committed and blood is drawn, it <u>automatically</u> becomes a major penalty.

Double minors (lasting 4 minutes) are assessed in one of two cases:

- for an accidental infraction that resulted in injury
- for an attempt to injure a player without actual injury resulting

These are called for infractions that are between a minor and major penalty in seriousness. If the opposing team scores a goal while a player is serving a double minor, only one 2-minute penalty is subtracted from the total time he must serve.

<u>Major Penalties</u>

These are assessed for many of the same infractions that apply to minor penalties, where the referee judges that either a greater degree of violence or deliberate violence was used against an opponent. The penalized player spends 5 minutes in the penalty box and there is no premature return to the ice even if a goal is scored. A major penalty is automatically called for a minor penalty infraction that draws blood. *Fighting* and *spearing* are two infractions always calling for major penalties. If the same player is cited three times in one game for a major penalty, or for a single major penalty for *butt-ending, checking* from behind, *clipping,* cross-checking, hooking, slashing or spearing, he must leave the game and not return. In all cases, a substitute may come on the ice for this penalized player after 5 minutes.

Bench Minor Penalties

This type of penalty is called whenever anybody on the *bench* commits an infraction such as using improper language with an official, throwing something on the ice, improperly leaving the bench, or in any way interfering with the game or an official. It may also be assessed for an infraction relating to an improper change to the *starting lineup* or for illegal substitutions, such as having *too many men on the ice*. One of the players on the ice, other than the goalie, must spend 2 minutes in the penalty box. The coach of the penalized team designates which player will serve time.

Match Penalties

Such penalties are rare and are the most serious, calling for banishment from the game and a monetary fine. A player who deliberately attempts to injure another player must leave the game for its duration and be replaced by a substitute who must first serve 5 minutes in the penalty box. During this time, the penalized player's team must play shorthanded.

Misconduct Penalties

Misconduct penalties differ from all others in that they permit immediate substitution, and the penalized player's team does not play shorthanded. Banishment is generally for 10 minutes following the use of abusive language or gestures, *unsportsmanlike conduct*, the failure to follow an official's orders, gesturing disrespectfully to any person, showing disrespect for a ruling, knocking or shooting the puck out of the reach of an official who is retrieving it, throwing equipment into the playing area, banging the boards with the sticks, not proceeding directly to the penalty box when instructed to do so or ignoring a warning to stop trying to incite an opponent into incurring a penalty.

Serious misconduct or abuse of an official can result in a game misconduct, where a penalized player is banished for the rest of the game. A rule designed to reduce bench-clearing brawls, the *third-man-in rule*, states that the third player involved in a fight will be assessed a game misconduct, even if he was only trying to break up the fight. This penalty and an automatic suspension from future game(s) applies to the first or second player on a team to leave the bench during an altercation.

Penalty Shot

Although it is rarely called, the *penalty shot* is one of the most exciting plays in hockey. A lone attacking player is allowed to maneuver the puck from center ice towards the goalie in an attempt to score while all the other players are stationed at the sides of the rink in front of their own benches. The puck is placed in the *center face-off circle*, and the player can stickhandle it anywhere to set up his shot. Once he crosses the attacking blue line, however, he must continue forward toward the goal. Only one shot at the goal is allowed and a rebound shot does not count.

A penalty shot is usually awarded when a player is illegally prevented from a clear scoring opportunity, such as when he is illegally interfered with from behind as he is moving in on the goal unopposed, or when a defending player other than the goalie picks up or deliberately falls on the puck while it is in his own *goal crease*. It is generally the player who was fouled who must take the penalty shot, though in some instances the captain of the non-offending team is allowed to select any player on the ice to take the shot. In the past, the shooter of a penalty shot had the advantage, but today's goalies are able to stop the majority of these attempts. In fact, if the player taking the penalty shot is not accustomed to stickhandling or to shooting the puck, the penalized team may be happier facing a penalty shot than it would have been playing 2 minutes shorthanded.

Goalie Penalties

The *goalie* will generally remain in the game even if he commits a minor, major or misconduct penalty infraction. One of his teammates who is on the ice at the time of the infraction will go to the penalty box and serve the goalie's time. This player is designated by the coach or manager of the offending team. However, a goalie who commits 3 major penalties will get a game misconduct penalty and must leave the game like any other player. Likewise, a goalie who commits a match penalty must also leave the game. In both cases, a substitute replaces the goalie. If a goalie holds onto a puck for more than 3 seconds when there are no opposing players around to check him, or if he intentionally bats the puck out of the rink with his stick, he will be called for a minor penalty called *delay of game*. A minor penalty will also be assessed if he leaves the immediate vicinity of his crease during an altercation.

Coincidental Penalties
Coincidental penalties occur when an equal number of players on opposing teams receive major or minor penalties at the same time. When only one minor penalty is called on each team, the players serve their time without substitution like a normal minor penalty. However, when coincidental minor penalties are called on more than one player on each team, when there are players already in the penalty box from either team, or when the coincidental penalties both are major penalties, the penalties have the effect of cancelling each other out. Although these penalized players serve their time in the penalty box, substitutes immediately replace them on the ice. This is to prevent coincidental penalties from causing teams to skate with fewer than 4 players plus a goalie, or in the case of coincidental major penalties, to prevent teams from having to skate with only 4 players plus a goalie for a prolonged period of time. Once their penalty time has expired, the penalized players can return to the ice only <u>after</u> play has stopped for some other reason, to allow the substitute players to leave the ice.

A rule instituted in 2002 dictates that in the final 5 minutes of the third period, or anytime in overtime, if one major (or match) penalty is called on one team and one minor penalty is called on the opposing team during the same stoppage of play, only the 3-minute difference (between a 5-minute major and a 2-minute minor, 5-2=3) is served immediately by the player who committed the major (or match) infraction. Without this rule players might be encouraged to instigate a fight or jeopardize the safety of opposing players late in the game because even though both teams would send players to the penalty box, there would be too little time to enforce a full 5-minutes against the team that committed the more serious offense. With this rule, if Player A commits a major (e.g., instigating a fight) while opponent Player B commits a minor (e.g., roughing), only A goes to the penalty box for 3 minutes and only his team is forced to play shorthanded.

Delayed Whistle
You might wonder why some penalties are called immediately by the referee while others are delayed. When a team in *possession* of the puck commits a penalty, the whistle is blown and play is stopped immediately. But when a player on the team not controlling the puck commits an infraction, the referee will point to the offending player but will wait until the team in possession of the puck completes its play with either a goal, a loss of possession or a *freezing of the puck* before blowing his whistle and stopping play. The purpose of this delay is simply to allow a non-offending team in possession of the puck a chance to score a goal, if it can, without interruption. If the penalty is a minor, and the non-offending team scores a goal, the penalty will not be imposed on the offending team. Major penalties are imposed regardless of whether a goal is scored.

Common Individual Penalties
Below are described some of the most common offenses for which penalties are assessed against players. Each of these offenses results in a minor penalty enforced against the offending player, unless otherwise noted. Officials use different hand signals to communicate each of these, shown with a description in the chapter entitled **OFFICIALS' HAND SIGNALS**.

- Boarding: when a player violently thrusts an opponent into the boards by body checking, elbowing or tripping. Boarding that causes injury to the face or head of an opponent results in a major penalty and a game misconduct.

- Butt-ending: when a player uses the end of the shaft of his stick to jab at an opponent. It is penalized by a major penalty and a game misconduct. A mere attempt to butt-end results in a double minor penalty.

- Charging: a deliberate move of more than two steps to run into an opponent. Also, jumping into an opponent to check him. Note: there is a slight difference between legal checking and illegal charging; only a player with the puck, or one who just gave up the puck, can be checked, and officials will count the number of strides a player takes before he makes contact with an opponent he is checking. If more than 2 steps are taken before hitting an opponent with excessive speed or force, it is charging. A game misconduct is assessed for charging a goalie in his crease or for charging any player that results in a head or face injury.

- Clipping: the act of throwing the body across or below the knees of an opponent

- Cross-checking: when a player *stick checks* an opponent's body with both hands on the stick and no part of the stick on the ice (See **Figure 15**)

- Delay of game: imposed on a player or goalkeeper who purposely delays the game in any way, such as by shooting or batting the puck outside the playing area to stall for time or deliberately displacing the goalpost from its normal position

- Elbowing: when a player strikes an opponent with his elbow

Figure 15: Cross-checking.

- Falling on the puck: when a player (other than the goalie in his own crease being checked by an opponent) falls on the puck, gathers it close to his body or closes his hand around it.

- Fighting: fisticuffs between players resulting in a major penalty and sometimes a game misconduct. If the referee deems that one player instigated the fight, that player receives an additional minor and a 10-minute misconduct penalty. A player who removes his jersey before a fight automatically receives an additional minor penalty and a game misconduct.

- High-Sticking: when a player checks an opponent with his stick above the height of his opponent's shoulders

- Holding: when one player holds onto or wraps his arms around an opponent or the opponent's stick to impede his progress

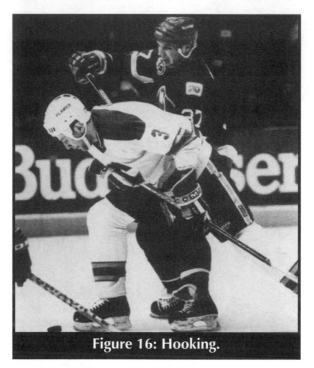

Figure 16: Hooking.

- Hooking: when a player attempts to impede the progress of another player by hooking him with the blade of his stick (See **Figure 16**)

- Interference: when a player attempts to impede the motion of another player not in possession of the puck. Interference is not called against a player who stands his ground against an oncoming opponent or a player who blocks an opponent while skating alongside him. In recent years, the NHL has urged officials to be more aggressive in enforcing this rule because skating free of obstructions is essential to the speed and fluidity of the game and its most skilled players.

- Kneeing: when a player strikes an opponent with his knee

- Roughing: shoving an opponent or involvement in a minor altercation or scuffle; a less severe form of fighting

Figure 17: Spearing.

- Slashing: when a player swings his stick aggressively in a slashing motion at an opponent

- Spearing: when a player thrusts his stick at an opponent in a stabbing motion (See **Figure 17**)

- Too many men on the ice: can occur when an entering substitute touches a puck possessed by the opposing team or makes any physical contact with an opposing player before a retiring teammate has completely left the ice

- Tripping: when a player trips an opponent with his stick or part of his body. A penalty is not called against a player who gains possession of the puck by using his stick in a hooking motion that ends up tripping an opponent. If a player trips an attacking opponent skating towards the goalie unopposed (with no defender between him and the goal, called a *breakaway*), a penalty shot is awarded to the opponent.

Now that you have learned the basics of ice hockey, it is time to explore some of the finer points of hockey strategy.

THINGS TO LOOK FOR DURING PLAY / STRATEGY

Hockey is a sport which can be difficult to understand because of its fast action and unique rules. However, with some basic knowledge of what to look for, you will be able to enjoy the strategy and hard-hitting action of this great sport.

WATCHING THE PUCK
Look for *caroms* or rebounds of the *puck*. In hockey, the puck often ricochets off the *boards* after hard shots or passes. In fact, hockey players use the boards like billiards players use the bumpers of a pool table. Therefore, when a player shoots the puck hard at one of the boards, look for the puck to be where a bounce off the boards would take it.

MATCH-UPS
A *match-up* is defined as a pairing of players on opposing teams who will *cover* each other during the hockey game. To cover a player is to stay close to prevent him from receiving a pass or making a play on offense. These pairings are vital, and *coaches* are always trying to get the edge on the other team by exploiting an opposing player's known weaknesses. An *NHL* rule requires the visiting team to name its *starting lineup* first to give the home team an advantage, allowing it to respond with the players on *forward* and *defensive lines* it feels are best suited to handle the visitors' lineup. The *referees* always allow the home team the option of making the final change of players, not only at the start of a *period*, but prior to any *face-off* as well. That is why you will often see referees order certain players off the ice before a face-off, ruling that the visiting team may not make any more changes.

ATTACK PATTERNS
In hockey, players can quickly skate from one end of the *rink* to another. Therefore, when a player has control of the puck,

he can quickly develop a chance to score a *goal* by skating toward the opponent's goal with his teammates. This is called a *break* or *rush*, and often catches the defense off-guard with little time to skate backwards into position.

Situations develop where the players on the attacking team (*offense*) may outnumber their opponents in the *attacking zone*. For example, if 2 attackers are defended by only 1 defenseman (in addition to the goalie) on a break, this is called a *2-on-1 break*. There are also *2-on-2* and *3-on-1* breaks. The more outnumbered the defenders are, the greater the chance is that the attacking team will have a man *open* for a *shot on goal*. An open player is one that is not covered by any defenders.

The extreme example of the break is the *breakaway*, where an attacker with the puck skates undefended towards the goal. This situation is similar to a *penalty shot* in that it pits a sole attacker against the goaltender in a one-on-one showdown.

ATTACK STRATEGIES
The attacking team will often try the following strategies to improve its chances of scoring:

Dumping The Puck Into The Zone
Because of the *offside* rule, attacking players must be careful to stay out of the attacking zone until the puck has crossed the *blue line*. When one or more players from the attacking team are about to commit an offside by crossing the blue line ahead of the puck, their teammate with the puck will often *dump* or shoot the puck into the attacking zone, where they chase after it and hope to regain control. In an example shown in **Figure 18**, player A dumps the puck so teammates B and C can enter the *attacking zone* without being offside.

Deking
In hockey, *deking* is the art of faking used by the *puck carrier* to make a defending player think the puck carrier is going

to pass or move in a certain direction when he is not. Body control and stick-handling are the keys to successful deking. A player's chest usually gives his true intentions away and a good defender watches this and *body checks* his opponent there. There are three main types of dekes:

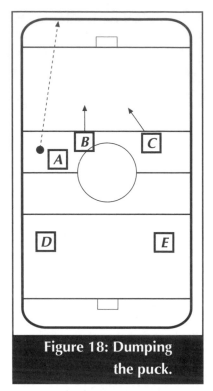

Figure 18: Dumping the puck.

- *Shoulder deke*: a quick move of the shoulder in one direction and the player in another.

- *Head deke*: when a player drops his head as though moving one way and quickly moves in another.

- *Stick deke*: when the *stick* is moved as though for a shot, but instead the player moves the puck past the defending player.

Where To Shoot The Puck In The Net

Players usually try to shoot the puck towards areas of the *net* that are most difficult for the *goaltender* to defend. The five most popular locations that players aim for are the upper and lower left and right corners of the goal and between the goalie's legs, called the *five-hole*. (See **Figure 19**) Because a goalie is slower with his feet than with his hands, it is usually more effective to shoot in the lower corners where he can only use his feet and stick to stop shots. Shots towards the upper corners are often more easily fended off or caught by the goalie's quicker hands.

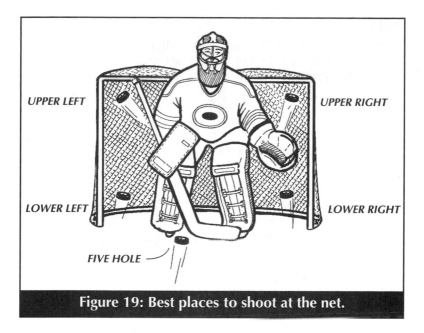

UPPER LEFT

UPPER RIGHT

LOWER LEFT

LOWER RIGHT

FIVE HOLE

Figure 19: Best places to shoot at the net.

These higher shots should be taken when the goalie is on his knees or lying on the ice and less able to defend the upper part of the goal.

Screening The Goalie
Goalies have extremely quick reactions, so they are able to stop shots they can see clearly from fairly short range. Therefore, players from the attacking team often try to stand in front of the goalie (although legally they must stay outside the *goal crease*) to partially block or *screen* his view. If the goalie cannot see the puck coming until the last instant, he has less time to react and make a *save*.

Deflections
The same players who screen the goalie are also in excellent position to use their sticks to *deflect* a shot or a pass into the net. A goalie anticipates the puck's flight from seeing the direction it takes off the shooter's stick, and often cannot react in time to stop a *deflection* that changes the puck's direction.

DEFENSE STRATEGY

Defending players try to stop attacking players any way they can. Defenders try to knock the puck away or physically disrupt the puck carrier so he loses control of the puck and his momentum. Good defenders do this with nimble skating, skillful use of the stick and hard *checking*.

Playing The Man / Checking

Rather than just trying to knock the puck away with their sticks, a much safer strategy for players on the defending team is to cover the player, checking him often and making sure he cannot get off a good pass or shot. Going just for the puck is riskier because if the defender misses the puck, the attacking player may get around the defender and have an open pass or shot on goal.

GOALIE STRATEGY: CUTTING DOWN THE ANGLE

When an attacker skates towards the goal with the puck, the goalie will often come out of the goal several feet to *cut down the angle* of the attacker's shot, leaving him with less *net* area to shoot at by making himself closer and larger to the shooter. (See **Figure 20**) However, this is risky because if an attacker maneuvers the puck past the forward-playing goalie, he has an open shot at the net.

POWER PLAYS

A *power play* is a critical juncture in a hockey game because it is an excellent scoring opportunity for the team with the extra player(s). This situation calls for some different strategies than the rest of the game when the teams are both at equal strength.

Power Play Set Up

The team that has an extra man or men (the team on the power play) tries to get set up in the attacking zone. Since it outnumbers the *shorthanded* team on the ice, it will always have at least one man that is open, or not defended. The best way for it to capitalize on this advantage is if all of its players are positioned in the attacking zone where they can

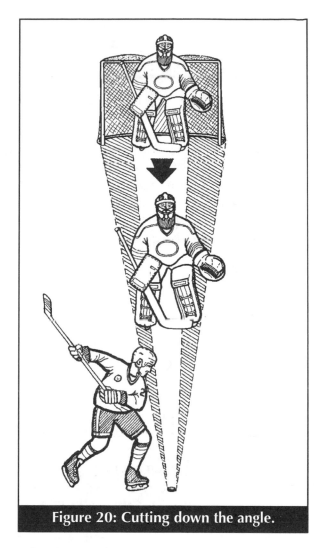

Figure 20: Cutting down the angle.

pass to each other and take shots at the goal. After setting up, players on the power play pass the puck around quickly to try to find the player with the best open shot. The two defensemen of that team set up at the *points* from which they can shoot at the net or pass to their teammates. The players at the points also help prevent the puck from leaving the zone. If the puck does leave the zone, to prevent an offside call, all the attacking players must *clear the zone*, or leave the attacking zone, before the puck can be brought back in.

<u>Shorthanded Strategy</u>

The team that has fewer players than the opposition, or the *shorthanded* team, tries to hold off the relentless attack of the opposition. It tries to regain control of the puck and keep it away from the team on the power play, allowing time on the penalty to wind down and expire, which is called *killing the penalty*. When the opposition is set up in its attacking zone, the shorthanded team always tries to *clear the puck*, or shoot it out of its *defending zone*, forcing the opposition to restart its power play set up all over again. A shorthanded team cannot be called for *icing*, so its players will not hesitate to slap the puck out of their own zone as hard as they can. A goal scored by a shorthanded team is a rare and exciting occurrence.

PULLING THE GOALIE

When a team is losing by only 1 or 2 goals near the end of a game and needs to score desperately, it will often remove or *pull the goalie* from the game and replace him with a skating player who can help with the attack. This other player has none of the privileges of the goalie; for example, he cannot handle the puck freely and is not protected from contact. This desperation tactic is used by a team to get more scoring power on the ice in the final moments of the game so it can catch up, but leaves the team's own net unguarded. Such a wide-open net may give the other team an opportunity to score easily if it regains possession of the puck. This type of goal is called an *empty-net goal*.

An NHL rule adopted in 2002 dictates that any team which pulls the goalie in overtime and loses the game forfeits the one *point* in the *standings* that it had automatically earned for being tied at the end of *regulation*. Without this rule, teams that were assured of this point were encouraged to risk pulling the goalie to improve their chances of scoring and earning a second point for a win. In addition, a goalie pulled in overtime cannot return to the ice until the next stoppage of play.

NHL TEAMS, DIVISIONS and CONFERENCES

LEAGUE HISTORY

The *NHL* began in 1917 with 4 Canadian teams. Its size has changed many times over the years with the addition of teams (*expansion*) or as teams ceased operations and were dissolved. In 1942-43, only 6 teams were active and they made up the NHL for the next 24 years:

Boston Bruins	*Montreal Canadiens*
Chicago Blackhawks	New York Rangers
Detroit Red Wings	Toronto Maple Leafs

In 1967, expansion added 6 teams bringing the total to 12, divided into the East and West *divisions*. Six more teams were added over the next 7 years, and in 1974 the NHL was reorganized into the *Prince of Wales* and *Clarence Campbell Conferences*. It was not until 1973-74 that an expansion team, the Philadelphia Flyers, won a *Stanley Cup*. Four more teams were absorbed into the league in 1979 when the defunct *World Hockey Association (WHA)* merged with the NHL, bringing the total to 21.

The next wave of expansion did not come until the 1990s when 5 more teams were added to the NHL, establishing professional hockey for the first time in areas of the Southeastern and Western U.S. Teams began playing in Anaheim, California (Mighty Ducks), Florida (Panthers), Tampa (Lightning), San Jose (Sharks), and Ottawa (Senators). As part of this expansion, in 1993 the names of the NHL's divisions and conferences were changed to more accurately reflect the geographic regions represented by teams. The Wales Conference became the *Eastern Conference*, the Campbell Conference became the *Western Conference*, and the name of each division was changed (e.g., the *Patrick Division* became the Northeast Division).

RECENT EXPANSION

The late 1990s and the early 21st century brought yet further growth to the NHL. Between the 1998-99 and 2000-01 seasons, 4 new expansion teams were added, bringing the number of teams to 30. The expansion schedule was as follows:

Season Entered NHL	Team
1998-1999	Nashville Predators
1999-2000	Atlanta Thrashers
2000-2001	Columbus Blue Jackets
2000-2001	Minnesota Wild

To manage this growth, beginning with the 1998-99 season the NHL added 2 more divisions and *realigned* several teams to fit into the six 5-team divisions and 2 conferences shown below:

Eastern Conference
- *Atlantic Division*
- *Northeast Division*
- *Southeast Division*

Western Conference
- *Central Division*
- *Northwest Division*
- *Pacific Division*

Shown in **Table 1** is an alphabetized list of the 30 NHL teams, the year they joined the NHL, and their divisions and conferences.

An example of how NHL teams are listed in the newspaper by division and conference is located in the chapter entitled **DECIPHERING HOCKEY STATISTICS IN THE NEWSPAPER**.

TABLE 1: NHL TEAMS

Team	Year	Pre-1993 Division	Pre-1993 Conference	Realigned Division	Realigned Conference
Anaheim Mighty Ducks	1993	—	—	Pacific	Western
Atlanta Thrashers	1999	—	—	Southeast	Eastern
Boston Bruins	1924	Adams	Wales	Northeast	Eastern
Buffalo Sabres	1970	Adams	Wales	Northeast	Eastern
Calgary Flames[1]	1972	Smythe	Campbell	Northwest	Western
Carolina Hurricanes[2,3]	1979	Adams	Wales	Southeast	Eastern
Chicago Blackhawks	1926	Norris	Campbell	Central	Western
Colorado Avalanche[3,4]	1979	Adams	Wales	Northwest	Western
Columbus Blue Jackets	2000	—	—	Central	Western
Dallas Stars[5]	1967	Norris	Campbell	Pacific	Western
Detroit Red Wings	1926	Norris	Campbell	Central	Western
Edmonton Oilers[3]	1979	Smythe	Campbell	Northwest	Western
Florida Panthers	1993	—	—	Southeast	Eastern
Los Angeles Kings	1967	Smythe	Campbell	Pacific	Western
Minnesota Wild	2000	—	—	Northwest	Western
Montreal Canadiens	1917	Adams	Wales	Northeast	Eastern
Nashville Predators	1998	—	—	Central	Western
New Jersey Devils[6]	1974	Patrick	Wales	Atlantic	Eastern
New York Islanders	1972	Patrick	Wales	Atlantic	Eastern
New York Rangers	1926	Patrick	Wales	Atlantic	Eastern
Ottawa Senators	1992	Adams	Wales	Northeast	Eastern
Philadelphia Flyers	1967	Patrick	Wales	Atlantic	Eastern
Phoenix Coyotes[3,7]	1979	Smythe	Campbell	Pacific	Western
Pittsburgh Penguins	1967	Patrick	Wales	Atlantic	Eastern
San Jose Sharks	1991	Smythe	Campbell	Pacific	Western
St. Louis Blues	1967	Norris	Campbell	Central	Western
Tampa Bay Lightning	1992	Norris	Campbell	Southeast	Eastern
Toronto Maple Leafs	1917	Norris	Campbell	Northeast	Eastern
Vancouver Canucks	1970	Smythe	Campbell	Northwest	Western
Washington Capitals	1974	Patrick	Wales	Southeast	Eastern

[1] transferred from Atlanta in 1980
[2] were the Hartford Whalers until 1997
[3] began in the WHA in 1972 and were absorbed into the NHL through the 1979 merger
[4] were the Quebec Nordiques until 1995
[5] were the Minnesota North Stars until 1993
[6] originated in Kansas City; were the Colorado Rockies 1976-82
[7] were the Winnipeg Jets until 1996

NHL SEASON, PLAYOFFS and THE STANLEY CUP

REGULAR SEASON
The *regular season* for *NHL* hockey is 82 games long. A season is referred to as the 2003-04 season, for example, because it starts the first week in October in one year and ends in mid-April of the following calendar year. A team usually plays half of its games at home and half on the road.

During regular-season play, NHL teams compete for the top spots in the *standings*. Teams are ranked within each *division* based on a simple *point* system:
- A team receives 2 points for each game it wins
- A team receives 1 point for each game that ends still *tied* after a 5-minute *overtime* is played
- A team receives 1 point for each tied game that it loses in overtime, called an *overtime loss*. This category was added starting with the 1999-2000 season. Before then, all losses were worth zero points
- Zero points are awarded for games lost in *regulation* (after 3 periods)

The more points a team has, the higher it is ranked; first place is the highest position (*division leader*), followed by second place, etc. Teams can be tied for a ranking. A team's record will be described by four numbers at any given point during a season, denoting *wins-losses-ties-overtime losses* (for example 40-15-4-2). The total of these four numbers is the number of games a team has played thus far in the season; in our example it would be 61 games.

PLAYOFFS
After the regular-season schedule of games is over, 16 teams will advance to the *post-season*, otherwise known as the *Stanley Cup playoffs*. The schedules for the playoffs will vary each year depending on how long each *round* lasts, but

generally the playoffs begin in mid-April and end in early June. When there were fewer teams in the NHL some critics complained that so many teams were rewarded with playoff berths that it made the regular season less meaningful. As the NHL has expanded, this criticism has decreased.

The top 8 teams in each of the 2 *conferences* make the playoffs. There are 4 rounds of playoffs used to narrow the number of teams by eliminating the losers of each round. Teams are paired up to play a *best-of-seven series* in each of the rounds. A best-of-seven game format means the first team to win 4 games emerges victorious. This can be done in as few as 4 games or in 5, 6 or 7 games. Over a seven-game series there is less chance that a weaker team can get lucky and advance to the next round than if only a single game were played.

The 3 division champions in each conference automatically qualify for the playoffs and are seeded #1 through #3 according to their regular-season record. The teams with the next 5 best records in each conference also qualify and are seeded #4 through #8.

In the first round the #1 team from each conference plays against the #8 team in the same conference, #2 vs. #7, #3 vs. #6, and #4 vs. #5. A total of eight first round series will be played, four in each conference. The winners of these first round series then play each other in the second round, called the Conference Semifinals, as shown in the diagram of playoff brackets. (See **Figure 21**) The third round is the Conference Finals that determines the champion of each conference. To honor the builders of hockey, the winners of the Eastern Conference receive the *Prince of Wales Trophy* and the winners of the Western Conference receive the *Campbell Bowl* as rewards for their victories.

These two conference champions then meet for the fourth, or final round which is called the *Stanley Cup finals*, to determine the best team in the NHL. The winners of the

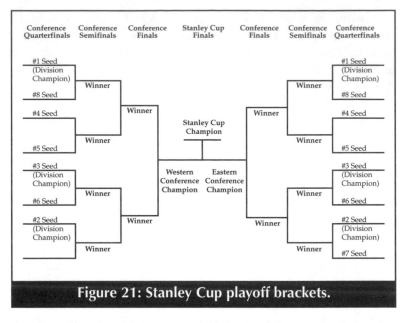

Conference Quarterfinals	Conference Semifinals	Conference Finals	Stanley Cup Finals	Conference Finals	Conference Semifinals	Conference Quarterfinals

#1 Seed (Division Champion)

#8 Seed

Winner

#4 Seed

Winner

#5 Seed

Winner

Stanley Cup Champion

Winner

#1 Seed (Division Champion)

#8 Seed

Winner

#4 Seed

Winner

#5 Seed

#3 Seed (Division Champion)

#6 Seed

Winner

Western Conference Champion

Eastern Conference Champion

#3 Seed (Division Champion)

#6 Seed

Winner

#2 Seed (Division Champion)

Winner

Winner

Winner

#2 Seed (Division Champion)

#7 Seed

Winner

Figure 21: Stanley Cup playoff brackets.

Stanley Cup finals are awarded the highly-coveted *Stanley Cup*, a silver trophy that stands 3 feet high, engraved with the names of each member of every Stanley Cup championship team. (See **Figure 22**) It is the oldest trophy competed for by professional athletes in North America. The Stanley Cup is held by one team until a new champion claims it. Although there can be a new champion every year, some teams throughout history have established dynasties, reclaiming the Cup several years in succession, such as the *Montreal Canadiens*, the Edmonton Oilers, the Toronto Maple Leafs and the New York Islanders.

HISTORY OF THE STANLEY CUP

In 1893, Canada's Governor-General, Sir Frederick Arthur, also known as Lord Stanley of Preston, bought a large trophy to give to an amateur hockey club in Montreal. He used his own pocket money to buy the silver cup, spending 10 pounds (or about $50 in American money). He placed this cup in the hands of a board of trustees to award it to the amateur hockey champions of Canada each year. However, as the sport of hockey grew in popularity, semipro and then professional teams were formed, and the trustees decided to make the cup an international hockey prize. Unfortunately for Lord Stanley, his term of office expired in May 1893, and he returned to England 10 months before the first-ever hockey playoffs were played, having never seen a single Stanley Cup game.

Winners of the Stanley Cup receive the trophy right on the ice after their final victory, and

Figure 22: The Stanley Cup.

their *captain* usually skates around the rink holding the Cup above his head. Despite its status, the Stanley Cup has had to be retrieved from assorted unusual locations: it has been thrown into a river, tossed over a graveyard fence, used as a flowerpot by an unsuspecting housewife, forgotten on the side of the road after the changing of a flat tire, and even stolen from the Chicago Stadium showcase by a Montreal fan who felt it belonged back in Montreal.

Although that fan was mistaken, the city of Montreal is indeed rich in Stanley Cup tradition. The first Stanley Cup match was held there on March 22, 1894 with the Montreal AAA's defeating the Ottawa Capitals by a score of 3-1. Since 1923 the Montreal Canadiens have won the cup 24 times, an incredible record of domination that is not likely to be broken anytime soon. The teams with the next-most Stanley Cup titles to their names are the Toronto Maple Leafs with 13 and the Detroit Red Wings with 10.

Some of the most memorable Stanley Cup finals include the 1919 championship which ended with no decision because of a flu epidemic; the longest game in hockey history was played in the 1936 series, a scoreless game that lasted 176 minutes and 30 seconds into the 6th overtime before the winning *goal* was scored; the 1942 series in which Detroit, despite having won the first 3 games, lost the next 4 in a row and the series to Toronto; the 1951 series in which every one of the 5 games it took for Toronto to beat Montreal went into overtime; the 1987 series in which the underdog Philadelphia Flyers rallied from a 3-1 deficit in games and a 3-1 score in Game 5 to tie the series 3-3 against the mighty Edmonton Oilers, only to lose the decisive Game 7; and the 2000 series won by the New Jersey Devils over the defending champion Dallas Stars where the series finished up with dramatic back-to-back triple-overtime and double-overtime games.

Since 1927, the year the Stanley Cup first became an exclusively NHL award, the trophy has been won by the teams listed in **Table 2**:

TABLE 2: STANLEY CUP FINALS

Season	Winner	Loser	Games
1926-27	Ottawa Senators	Boston Bruins	2-0
1927-28	New York Rangers	Montreal Maroons	3-2
1928-29	Boston Bruins	New York Rangers	2-0
1929-30	Montreal Canadiens	Boston Bruins	2-0
1930-31	Montreal Canadiens	Chicago Blackhawks	3-2
1931-32	Toronto Maple Leafs	New York Rangers	3-0
1932-33	New York Rangers	Toronto Maple Leafs	3-1
1933-34	Chicago Blackhawks	Detroit Red Wings	3-1
1934-35	Montreal Maroons	Toronto Maple Leafs	3-0
1935-36	Detroit Red Wings	Toronto Maple Leafs	3-1
1936-37	Detroit Red Wings	New York Rangers	3-2
1937-38	Chicago Blackhawks	Toronto Maple Leafs	3-1
1938-39	Boston Bruins	Toronto Maple Leafs	4-1
1939-40	New York Rangers	Toronto Maple Leafs	4-2
1940-41	Boston Bruins	Detroit Red Wings	4-0
1941-42	Toronto Maple Leafs	Detroit Red Wings	4-3
1942-43	Detroit Red Wings	Boston Bruins	4-0
1943-44	Montreal Canadiens	Chicago Blackhawks	4-0
1944-45	Toronto Maple Leafs	Detroit Red Wings	4-3
1945-46	Montreal Canadiens	Boston Bruins	4-1
1946-47	Toronto Maple Leafs	Montreal Canadiens	4-2
1947-48	Toronto Maple Leafs	Detroit Red Wings	4-0
1948-49	Toronto Maple Leafs	Detroit Red Wings	4-0
1949-50	Detroit Red Wings	New York Rangers	4-3
1950-51	Toronto Maple Leafs	Montreal Canadiens	4-1
1951-52	Detroit Red Wings	Montreal Canadiens	4-0
1952-53	Montreal Canadiens	Boston Bruins	4-1
1953-54	Detroit Red Wings	Montreal Canadiens	4-3
1954-55	Detroit Red Wings	Montreal Canadiens	4-3
1955-56	Montreal Canadiens	Detroit Red Wings	4-1
1956-57	Montreal Canadiens	Boston Bruins	4-1
1957-58	Montreal Canadiens	Boston Bruins	4-2
1958-59	Montreal Canadiens	Toronto Maple Leafs	4-1
1959-60	Montreal Canadiens	Toronto Maple Leafs	4-0
1960-61	Chicago Blackhawks	Detroit Red Wings	4-2
1961-62	Toronto Maple Leafs	Chicago Blackhawks	4-2
1962-63	Toronto Maple Leafs	Detroit Red Wings	4-1

Season	Winner	Loser	Games
1963-64	Toronto Maple Leafs	Detroit Red Wings	4-3
1964-65	Montreal Canadiens	Chicago Blackhawks	4-3
1965-66	Montreal Canadiens	Detroit Red Wings	4-2
1966-67	Toronto Maple Leafs	Montreal Canadiens	4-2
1967-68	Montreal Canadiens	St. Louis Blues	4-0
1968-69	Montreal Canadiens	St. Louis Blues	4-0
1969-70	Boston Bruins	St. Louis Blues	4-0
1970-71	Montreal Canadiens	Chicago Blackhawks	4-3
1971-72	Boston Bruins	New York Rangers	4-2
1972-73	Montreal Canadiens	Chicago Blackhawks	4-2
1973-74	Philadelphia Flyers	Boston Bruins	4-2
1974-75	Philadelphia Flyers	Buffalo Sabres	4-2
1975-76	Montreal Canadiens	Philadelphia Flyers	4-0
1976-77	Montreal Canadiens	Boston Bruins	4-0
1977-78	Montreal Canadiens	Boston Bruins	4-2
1978-79	Montreal Canadiens	New York Rangers	4-1
1979-80	New York Islanders	Philadelphia Flyers	4-2
1980-81	New York Islanders	Minnesota North Stars	4-1
1981-82	New York Islanders	Vancouver Canucks	4-0
1982-83	New York Islanders	Edmonton Oilers	4-0
1983-84	Edmonton Oilers	New York Islanders	4-1
1984-85	Edmonton Oilers	Philadelphia Flyers	4-1
1985-86	Montreal Canadiens	Calgary Flames	4-1
1986-87	Edmonton Oilers	Philadelphia Flyers	4-3
1987-88	Edmonton Oilers	Boston Bruins	4-0
1988-89	Calgary Flames	Montreal Canadiens	4-2
1989-90	Edmonton Oilers	Boston Bruins	4-1
1990-91	Pittsburgh Penguins	Minnesota North Stars	4-2
1991-92	Pittsburgh Penguins	Chicago Blackhawks	4-0
1992-93	Montreal Canadiens	Los Angeles Kings	4-1
1993-94	New York Rangers	Vancouver Canucks	4-3
1994-95	New Jersey Devils	Detroit Red Wings	4-0
1995-96	Colorado Avalanche	Florida Panthers	4-0
1996-97	Detroit Red Wings	Philadelphia Flyers	4-0
1997-98	Detroit Red Wings	Washington Capitals	4-0
1998-99	Dallas Stars	Buffalo Sabres	4-2
1999-00	New Jersey Devils	Dallas Stars	4-2
2000-01	Colorado Avalanche	New Jersey Devils	4-3
2001-02	Detroit Red Wings	Carolina Hurricanes	4-1

INDIVIDUAL STATISTICS

Various career and season statistics are kept for each individual *NHL* player to keep track of his performance. The explanations below will help you become familiar with these statistics so you will understand measures of success for hockey players. Some of these statistics are tabulated for the best hockey players of all-time in the chapter entitled **NHL INDIVIDUAL RECORDS**.

GAMES PLAYED (GP): The number of games a player appeared in, even if only for a few minutes.

GOALS (G): The number of times a player shoots the *puck* across the *goal line* between the *goalposts*.

ASSISTS (A): The number of times a player passes to a teammate who either scores or passes to another teammate who scores. A player who scores a goal cannot also be credited with an assist on the same goal.

POINTS (Pts): The number of goals plus the number of assists for a player.

PLUS/MINUS (+/-): This statistic indicates the overall success of a player's team while he is on the ice. It is calculated by giving a player a "plus" (+1) when he is on the ice when an even-strength or shorthanded goal is scored by his team, and a "minus" (-1) when he is on the ice for an even-strength or shorthanded goal scored by the opposing team. These pluses and minuses are all added together to get the plus/minus statistic.

PENALTY MINUTES (PIM): The total amount of penalty time assessed to a player.

POWER PLAY GOALS (PP): The number of goals scored by a player when his team is on the *power play*.

SHORTHANDED GOALS (SH): The number of goals scored by a player when his team is *shorthanded*.

GAME-WINNING GOALS (GW): The number of times a player scored a goal that put his team ahead for good.

GAME-TYING GOALS (GT): The number of times a player scored a goal to tie the score where the teams remained tied.

SHOTS ON GOAL (SOG or S): A scoring attempt that either results in a goal, or is successfully blocked or otherwise prevented by a *goalie* (called a *save*).

SHOOTING PERCENTAGE (% or PCT): The proportion of a player's shots on goal that result in goals. Calculated by dividing goals by shots on goal (G/SOG).

GOALS AGAINST (GA): The total number of goals a goalie has allowed other teams to score while he was protecting the goal.

GOALS-AGAINST AVERAGE (Avg.): Calculated by dividing goals against for a goalie, excluding *empty-net goals*, by the number of minutes he played, and multiplying the result by 60, the number of minutes in a full game (GA/minutes x 60). The lower this number, the better.

SAVES (SV): The number of shots on goal a goalie prevented from going in the *net*.

SHOTS AGAINST (SA): The number of shots on goal against a goalie.

SAVE PERCENTAGE (S% or SPCT): The percentage of shot attempts a goalie successfully prevented, calculated by dividing the number of saves by shots against (SV/SA).

SHUTOUTS (SO): The number of times a goalie has played a complete game without allowing any goals to be scored.

DECIPHERING HOCKEY STATISTICS IN THE NEWSPAPER

Each day during the hockey season, most major newspapers contain lots of information about *NHL* hockey teams and players. There are team *standings*, showing how each team is performing in terms of wins and losses, and there are summaries of each game played the previous day called *game summaries* or *box scores*.

This section discusses how the team standings and game summaries appear in the newspaper.

TEAM STANDINGS: The team standings list each of the teams by total *points* earned during the season. Points are earned as follows:

- A team receives 2 points for each game it wins
- A team receives 1 point for each game that ends still *tied* after a 5-minute *overtime* is played
- A team receives 1 point for each tied game that it loses in overtime, called an *overtime loss*. This category was added starting with the 1999-2000 season. Before then, all losses were worth zero points.
- Zero points are awarded for games lost in *regulation* (after 3 periods)

The information contained in these standings is described on the following page, using actual NHL standings as an example.

L - The number of losses a team has so far in the season.

W - The number of wins a team has so far in the season.

OTL - The number of overtime losses a team has so far in the season.

T - The number of ties a team has so far in the season.

Pts - Points earned by a team during the season to date.

Div. - A team's win-loss-tie record when it plays other teams in its division. Teams play more frequently against teams within their division than outside. Therefore, this statistic usually measures how well a team plays against its biggest rivals.

Home/Away - A team's win-loss-tie record when it plays on its home ice or on the road.

Eastern Conference

Atlantic Division	W	L	T	OTL	Pts	GF	GA	Home	Away	Div.
Philadelphia	42	27	10	3	97	234	192	20-16-5	22-14-5	10-8-2
N.Y. Islanders	42	28	8	4	96	239	220	21-15-5	21-17-3	11-8-1
New Jersey	41	28	9	4	95	205	187	22-15-4	19-17-5	10-8-2
N.Y. Rangers	36	38	4	4	80	227	258	19-20-2	17-22-2	7-12-1
Pittsburgh	28	41	8	5	69	198	249	16-21-4	12-25-4	8-10-2

Northeast Division	W	L	T	OTL	Pts	GF	GA	Home	Away	Div.
Boston	43	24	6	9	101	236	201	23-16-2	20-17-4	9-10-1
Toronto	43	25	10	4	100	249	207	24-11-6	19-18-4	10-5-5
Ottawa	39	27	9	7	94	243	208	21-17-3	18-17-6	8-11-1
Montreal	36	31	12	3	87	207	209	21-14-6	15-20-6	6-10-4
Buffalo	35	35	11	1	82	213	200	20-16-5	15-20-6	10-7-3

Southeast Division	W	L	T	OTL	Pts	GF	GA	Home	Away	Div.
Carolina	35	26	16	5	91	217	217	15-15-11	20-16-5	11-4-5
Washington	36	33	11	2	85	228	240	21-14-6	15-21-5	12-4-4
Tampa Bay	27	40	11	4	69	178	219	16-20-5	11-24-6	7-10-3
Florida	22	44	10	6	60	180	250	11-27-3	11-23-7	5-12-3
Atlanta	19	47	11	5	54	187	288	11-21-9	8-31-2	4-9-7

GF - Goals For, or total goals scored by a team. An indicator of a team's offensive strength.

GA - Goals Against, or total goals scored against a team. An indicator of a team's defensive strength.

Western Conference

Central Division	W	L	T	OTL	Pts	GF	GA	Home	Away	Div.
Detroit	51	17	10	4	116	251	187	28-8-5	23-13-5	10-6-4
St. Louis	43	27	8	4	98	227	188	27-13-1	16-18-7	10-7-3
Chicago	41	27	13	1	96	216	207	28-8-5	13-20-8	9-6-5
Nashville	28	41	13	0	69	196	230	17-16-8	11-25-5	7-10-3
Columbus	22	47	8	5	57	164	255	14-22-5	8-30-3	5-12-3

Northwest Division	W	L	T	OTL	Pts	GF	GA	Home	Away	Div.
Colorado	45	28	8	1	99	212	169	24-13-4	21-16-4	10-6-4
Vancouver	42	30	7	3	94	254	211	23-13-5	19-20-2	10-8-2
Edmonton	38	28	12	4	92	205	182	23-14-4	15-18-8	10-5-5
Calgary	32	35	12	3	79	201	220	20-16-5	12-22-7	8-8-4
Minnesota	26	35	12	9	73	195	238	14-19-8	12-25-4	4-15-1

Pacific Division	W	L	T	OTL	Pts	GF	GA	Home	Away	Div.
San Jose	44	27	8	3	99	248	199	25-13-3	19-17-5	10-9-1
Los Angeles	40	27	11	4	95	214	190	22-13-6	18-18-5	10-6-4
Phoenix	40	27	9	6	95	228	210	27-11-3	13-22-6	7-10-3
Dallas	36	28	13	5	90	215	213	18-17-6	18-16-7	9-9-2
Anaheim	29	42	8	3	69	175	198	15-21-5	14-24-3	8-10-2

GAME SUMMARIES: Being able to read a game summary or box score allows a reader to re-create the action and sequence of events that took place during a hockey game. There are several pieces of information contained in a box score, as explained below:

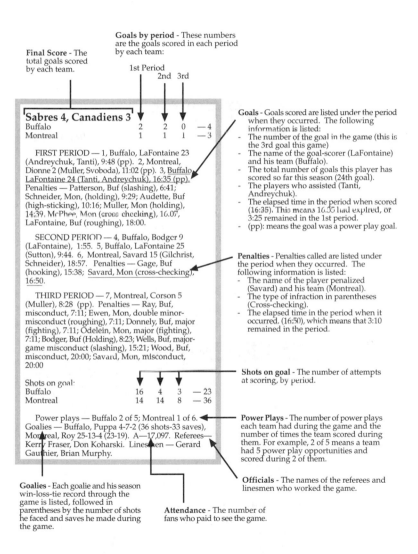

Final Score - The total goals scored by each team.

Goals by period - These numbers are the goals scored in each period by each team:

1st Period
2nd 3rd

Sabres 4, Canadiens 3
Buffalo   2   2   0   — 4
Montreal   1   1   1   — 3

FIRST PERIOD — 1, Buffalo, LaFontaine 23 (Andreychuk, Tanti), 9:48 (pp). 2, Montreal, Dionne 2 (Muller, Svoboda), 11:02 (pp). 3, Buffalo, LaFontaine 24 (Tanti, Andreychuk), 16:35 (pp). Penalties — Patterson, Buf (slashing), 6:41; Schneider, Mon, (holding), 9:29; Audette, Buf (high-sticking), 10:16; Muller, Mon (holding), 14:39, McPhee, Mon (cross checking), 16.07, LaFontaine, Buf (roughing), 18:00.

SECOND PERIOD — 4, Buffalo, Bodger 9 (LaFontaine), 1:55. 5, Buffalo, LaFontaine 25 (Sutton), 9:44. 6, Montreal, Savard 15 (Gilchrist, Schneider), 18:57. Penalties — Gage, Buf (hooking), 15:38; Savard, Mon (cross-checking), 16:50.

THIRD PERIOD — 7, Montreal, Corson 5 (Muller), 8:28 (pp). Penalties — Ray, Buf, misconduct, 7:11; Ewen, Mon, double minor-misconduct (roughing), 7:11; Donnely, Buf, major (fighting), 7:11; Odelein, Mon, major (fighting), 7:11; Bodger, Buf (Holding), 8:23; Wells, Buf, major-game misconduct (slashing), 15:21; Wood, Buf, misconduct, 20:00; Savard, Mon, misconduct, 20:00.

Shots on goal·
Buffalo   16   4   3   — 23
Montreal   14   14   8   — 36

Power plays — Buffalo 2 of 5; Montreal 1 of 6. Goalies — Buffalo, Puppa 4-7-2 (36 shots-33 saves), Montreal, Roy 25-13-4 (23-19). A—17,097. Referees—Kerry Fraser, Don Koharski. Linesmen — Gerard Gauthier, Brian Murphy.

Goals - Goals scored are listed under the period when they occurred. The following information is listed:
- The number of the goal in the game (this is the 3rd goal this game)
- The name of the goal-scorer (LaFontaine) and his team (Buffalo).
- The total number of goals this player has scored so far this season (24th goal).
- The players who assisted (Tanti, Andreychuk).
- The elapsed time in the period when scored (16:35). This means 16.35 had expired, or 3:25 remained in the 1st period.
- (pp): means the goal was a power play goal.

Penalties - Penalties called are listed under the period when they occurred. The following information is listed:
- The name of the player penalized (Savard) and his team (Montreal).
- The type of infraction in parentheses (Cross-checking).
- The elapsed time in the period when it occurred. (16:50), which means that 3:10 remained in the period.

Shots on goal - The number of attempts at scoring, by period.

Power Plays - The number of power plays each team had during the game and the number of times the team scored during them. For example, 2 of 5 means a team had 5 power play opportunities and scored during 2 of them.

Officials - The names of the referees and linesmen who worked the game.

Goalies - Each goalie and his season win-loss-tie record through the game is listed, followed in parentheses by the number of shots he faced and saves he made during the game.

Attendance - The number of fans who paid to see the game.

NHL INDIVIDUAL RECORDS
(Statistics current through end of 2001-02 season)
The following abbreviations will be used in this section:

A = assists   L = losses
Avg = average   Pts = points
Dec = decisions   SO = shutouts
G = goals   T = ties
GA = goals against   Yrs = years
GP = games played   * = active player

CAREER LEADERS

All-Time Career Goal-Scoring Leaders:

Player	Team	Yrs	GP	G
Wayne Gretzky	Edmonton, LA, StL, NYR	20	1,487	894
Gordie Howe	Detroit, Hartford	26	1,767	801
Marcel Dionne	Detroit, LA, NY Rangers	18	1,348	731
Phil Esposito	Chicago, Bos, NY Rangers	18	1,282	717
Michael Gartner	Wash, Min, NYR, Tor, Phx	19	1,432	708
Brett Hull*	Calgary, StL, Dallas, Det	17	1,101	679
Steve Yzerman*	Detroit	19	1,362	658
Mark Messier*	Edmonton, NYR, Van	23	1,602	658
Mario Lemieux*	Pittsburgh	14	812	654
Luc Robitaille*	LA, Pittsburgh, NYR	16	1,205	620
Bobby Hull	Chi, Winnipeg, Hartford	16	1,063	610

All-Time Career Assist Leaders:

Player	Team	Yrs	GP	A
Wayne Gretzky	Edmonton, LA, StL, NYR	20	1,487	1,963
Ron Francis*	Hartford, Pitt, Carolina	21	1,569	1,187
Ray Bourque	Boston, Colorado	22	1,612	1,169
Mark Messier*	Edmonton, NYR, Van	23	1,602	1,146
Paul Coffey	Edm, Pitt, LA, Det, Hfd, Phi, Chi, Carolina, Boston	21	1,409	1,135
Gordie Howe	Detroit, Hartford	26	1,767	1,049
Marcel Dionne	Detroit, LA, NY Rangers	18	1,348	1,040
Adam Oates*	Det, StL, Bos, Wash, Phi	17	1,210	1,027
Steve Yzerman*	Detroit	19	1,362	1,004
Mario Lemieux*	Pittsburgh	14	812	947
Doug Gilmour*	StL, Cgy, Tor, NJ, Chi, Buf, Mtl	19	1,412	945

All-Time Career Point Leaders:

Player	Team	Yrs	GP	G	A	Pts
Wayne Gretzky	Edm, LA, StL, NYR	20	1,487	894	1,963	2,857
Gordie Howe	Det, Hfd	26	1,767	801	1,049	1,850
Mark Messier*	Edmonton NYR, Van	23	1,602	658	1,146	1,804
Marcel Dionne	Det, LA, NYR	18	1,348	731	1,040	1,771
Ron Francis*	Hfd, Pitt, Car	21	1,569	514	1,187	1,701
Steve Yzerman*	Detroit	19	1,362	658	1,004	1,662
Mario Lemieux*	Pittsburgh	14	812	654	947	1,601
Phil Esposito	Chi, Bos, NYR	18	1,282	717	873	1,590
Ray Bourque	Boston, Colorado	22	1,612	410	1,169	1,579
Paul Coffey	Edm, Pitt, LA, Det, Hfd, Phi, Chi, Car, Bos	21	1,409	396	1,135	1,531
Stan Mikita	Chicago	22	1,394	541	926	1,467
Bryan Trottier	NYIsl, Pitt	18	1,279	524	901	1,425
Dale Hawerchuk	Win, Buf, StL, Phi	16	1,188	518	891	1,409

SINGLE-SEASON RECORDS

Individual Regular-Season Goal Leaders:

Player	Team	Season	G
Wayne Gretzky	Edmonton	'81-'82	92
Wayne Gretzky	Edmonton	'83-'84	87
Brett Hull*	St. Louis	'90-'91	86
Mario Lemieux*	Pittsburgh	'88-'89	85
Phil Esposito	Boston	'70-'71	76
Alexander Mogilny*	Buffalo	'92-'93	76
Teemu Selanne*	Winnepeg	'92-'93	76
Wayne Gretzky	Edmonton	'84-'85	73
Brett Hull*	St. Louis	'89-'90	72
Wayne Gretzky	Edmonton	'82-'83	71
Jari Kurri	Edmonton	'84-'85	71
Mario Lemieux*	Pittsburgh	'87-'88	70
Bernie Nicholls	Los Angeles	'88-'89	70
Brett Hull*	St. Louis	'91-'92	70

Individual Regular-Season Assist Leaders:

Player	Team	Season	A
Wayne Gretzky	Edmonton	'85-'86	163
Wayne Gretzky	Edmonton	'84-'85	135
Wayne Gretzky	Edmonton	'82-'83	125
Wayne Gretzky	Los Angeles	'90-'91	122
Wayne Gretzky	Edmonton	'86-'87	121
Wayne Gretzky	Edmonton	'81-'82	120
Wayne Gretzky	Edmonton	'83-'84	118
Wayne Gretzky	Los Angeles	'88-'89	114
Mario Lemieux*	Pittsburgh	'88-'89	114
Wayne Gretzky	Edmonton	'87-'88	109
Wayne Gretzky	Edmonton	'80-'81	109
Wayne Gretzky	Los Angeles	'89-'90	102
Bobby Orr	Boston	'70-'71	102

Individual Regular-Season Point Leaders:

Player	Team	Season	G	A	Pts
W. Gretzky	Edmonton	'85-'86	52	163	215
W. Gretzky	Edmonton	'81-'82	92	120	212
W. Gretzky	Edmonton	'84-'85	73	135	208
W. Gretzky	Edmonton	'83-'84	87	118	205
M. Lemieux*	Pittsburgh	'88-'89	85	114	199
W. Gretzky	Edmonton	'82-'83	71	125	196
W. Gretzky	Edmonton	'86-'87	62	121	183
M. Lemieux*	Pittsburgh	'87-'88	70	98	168
W. Gretzky	Los Angeles	'88-'89	54	114	168
W. Gretzky	Edmonton	'80-'81	55	109	164
W. Gretzky	Los Angeles	'90-'91	41	122	163
M. Lemieux*	Pittsburgh	'95-'96	69	92	161

PLAYOFF RECORDS

All-Time Playoff Goal Leaders:

Player	Team	Yrs	GP	G
Wayne Gretzky	Edmonton, LA, StL, NYR	16	208	122
Mark Messier*	Edmonton, NY Rangers	17	236	109
Jari Kurri	Edm, LA, NYR, Ana, Col	15	200	106
Brett Hull*	Calgary, St. Louis, Dal, Det	17	186	100
Glenn Anderson	Edmonton, Tor, NYR, StL	15	225	93
Mike Bossy	NY Islanders	10	129	85
Maurice Richard	Montreal	15	133	82
Claude Lemieux*	Montreal, NJ, Col, Phx	16	226	80
Jean Beliveau	Montreal	17	162	79
Mario Lemieux*	Pittsburgh	8	107	76
Dino Ciccarelli	Minn, Wash, Detroit	14	141	73
Esa Tikkanen	Edm, NYR, StL, Van, Wash	13	186	72
Bryan Trottier	NY Islanders, Pittsburgh	17	221	71

All-Time Playoff Assist Leaders:

Player	Team	Yrs	GP	A
Wayne Gretzky	Edmonton, LA, StL, NYR	16	208	260
Mark Messier*	Edmonton, NY Rangers	17	236	186
Ray Bourque	Boston, Colorado	21	214	139
Paul Coffey	Edm, Pitt, LA, Det, Phi, Car	16	194	137
Doug Gilmour*	StL, Calgary, Tor, NJ, Buf, Mtl	17	182	127
Jari Kurri	Edm, LA, NYR, Ana, Col	15	200	127
Glenn Anderson	Edmonton, Tor, NYR, StL	15	225	121
Al MacInnis*	Calgary, St. Louis	18	174	120
Larry Robinson	Montreal, Los Angeles	20	227	116
Larry Murphy	LA, Wash, Min, Pit, Tor, Det	20	215	115
Bryan Trottier	NY Islanders, Pittsburgh	17	221	113
Sergei Fedorov*	Detroit	12	158	111
Denis Savard	Chicago, Montreal	16	169	109

All-Time Playoff Point Leaders:

Player	Team	Yrs	GP	G	A	Pts
W. Gretzky	Edm, LA, StL, NYR	16	208	122	260	382
Mark Messier*	Edm, NYR	17	236	109	186	295
Jari Kurri	Edm, LA, NYR, Ana, Col	15	200	106	127	233
Glenn Anderson	Edm, Tor, NYR, StL	15	225	93	121	214
Paul Coffey	Edm, Pitt, LA, Detroit, Phi, Car	16	194	59	137	196
Doug Gilmour*	StL, Cgy, Tor, NJ, Buf, Mtl	17	182	60	127	187
Brett Hull*	Cgy, StL, Dal, Det	17	186	100	84	184
Bryan Trottier	NYI, Pitt	17	221	71	113	184
Ray Bourque	Boston, Col	21	214	41	139	180
Jean Beliveau	Montreal	17	162	79	97	176
Steve Yzerman*	Detroit	17	177	67	108	175
Denis Savard	Chi, Montreal	16	169	66	109	175
Mario Lemieux*	Pittsburgh	8	107	76	96	172

GOALTENDING STATISTICS

All-Time Shutout Leaders:

Player	Team	Yrs	GP	SO
Terry Sawchuk	Det, Bos, Tor, LA, NYR	21	971	103
G. Hainsworth	Montreal, Toronto	11	464	94
Glenn Hall	Detroit, Chicago, St. Louis	18	906	84
Jacques Plante	Mtl, NYR, StL, Tor, Bos	18	837	82
Tiny Thompson	Boston, Detroit	12	553	81
Alex Connell	Ott, Det, NYA, Maroons	12	417	81
Tony Esposito	Montreal, Chicago	16	886	76
Lorne Chabot	NYR, Tor, Montreal, Chi, Maroons, NY Americans	11	411	73
Harry Lumley	Det, NYR, Chi, Tor, Bos	16	804	71
Roy Worters	Pitt, NY Americans, Mtl	12	484	67
Turk Broda	Toronto	14	629	62

Single-Season Regular-Season Shutout Leaders:

Player	Team	Season	GP	SO
G. Hainsworth	Montreal	1928-29	44	22
Alex Connell	Ottawa	1925-26	36	15
Alex Connell	Ottawa	1927-28	44	15
Hal Winkler	Boston	1927-28	44	15
Tony Esposito	Chicago	1969-70	76	15
G. Hainsworth	Montreal	1926-27	44	14
Clint Benedict	Mtl. Maroons	1926-27	44	13
Alex Connell	Ottawa	1926-27	44	13
G. Hainsworth	Montreal	1927-28	44	13
John Roach	NY Rangers	1928-29	44	13
Roy Worters	NY Americans	1928-29	44	13
Harry Lumley	Toronto	1953-54	70	13
Dominik Hasek	Buffalo	1997-98	72	13

All-Time Win Leaders:

Player	Wins	GP	Dec	L	T	%
Patrick Roy*	516	966	934	300	118	.616
Terry Sawchuk	447	971	950	330	173	.562
Jacques Plante	435	837	827	247	145	.614
Tony Esposito	423	886	881	306	152	.567
Glenn Hall	407	906	897	327	163	.545
Grant Fuhr	403	868	812	295	114	.567
Mike Vernon*	385	781	750	273	92	.575
Andy Moog	372	713	669	209	88	.622
John Vanbiesbrouck	372	877	834	343	119	.517
Tom Barrasso*	368	771	727	273	86	.565
Ed Belfour*	364	735	706	242	100	.586

Single-Season Goals-Against Average Leaders since 1935:

Player	Team	Season	GP	GA	SO	Avg
Dave Kerr	NYR	1939-40	48	77	8	1.54
Frankie Brimsek	Boston	1938-39	43	68	10	1.56
Tiny Thompson	Boston	1935-36	48	82	10	1.68
Al Rollins	Toronto	1950-51	40	70	5	1.77
Tony Esposito	Chicago	1971-72	48	82	9	1.77
Ron Tugnutt*	Ottawa	1998-99	43	75	3	1.79
Lorne Chabot	Chicago	1934-35	48	88	8	1.80
Tiny Thompson	Boston	1937-38	48	89	7	1.80
Harry Lumley	Toronto	1953-54	69	128	13	1.86
Jacques Plante	Montreal	1955-56	64	119	7	1.86
Dominik Hasek	Buffalo	1998-99	64	119	9	1.87

THE NHL DRAFT

The *NHL draft* is held once a year in June, about 7-10 days after the last game of the *Stanley Cup finals*. Amateur hockey players from all over the world who are at least 18 years old before September 15th of the draft year can be selected by NHL teams. However, those players who will not have turned 19 by that date must inform the NHL in writing by May that they wish to "opt in" for that year's draft to be eligible. By doing so, they forfeit their remaining eligibility to play in NCAA collegiate games, so usually only serious NHL prospects decide to opt in.

The order of selection is in reverse order of the teams' *regular-season* records (ignoring the results of any *post-season* play). If any teams are *tied*, the tiebreakers include comparing their respective number of wins or the results of head-to-head play between the tied teams. To discourage teams from purposely losing games to end up with the worst record and the first pick, the NHL uses a weighted lottery system to determine the selection order for the 14 non-*playoff* teams. In this system, the team with the worst record during the regular season (the fewest *points*) has the greatest chance of winning the first pick (25%) and the 5th-worst team has the slimmest odds (8%). No team can move up more than 4 positions in the draft order due to the drawing, nor can it drop more than one spot.

There are currently 9 *rounds* in the draft; this means each team has the opportunity to select 9 players, one per round. There is a player that will be drafted "1st overall"; this means he was the first choice in the first round made by the NHL team that drafted first (or had the worst end-of-season record). This player is usually the best player of all those available that year, and he is expected to help the worst team improve in the next season and ultimately enhance the competition in the NHL. You might also hear a player referred to as "the Philadelphia Flyers' 1ˢᵗ pick in 2001"; this signifies the player was the first player chosen by that team, even if his team did not choose first within that round.

Whenever an *expansion team* is added to the league, a separate *expansion draft* is held. Existing teams are permitted to "protect" a certain number of their key players, but must leave most members of their team exposed. The expansion teams can then select from among the unprotected players to create their teams. This allows new teams to start their first season with some experienced and talented NHL players which helps them compete against the older, established teams in the league. Still it usually takes a few years for an expansion team to improve its season record. However, after a few years of doing poorly, an expansion team will have had several opportunities to draft high in the June draft, selecting from among the best young players each year. Such a team is likely to improve quickly.

NHL ALL-STAR GAME
& ALL-STAR TEAMS

ALL-STAR GAME
The *National Hockey League*'s annual *All-Star Game* is held in late January or early February, midway through the *regular season*. The game is generally played on a Saturday, and the location changes each year. Since 1998, the game has been played between the best players from the U.S. and Canada (North American All-Stars) and the best from the rest of the world (World All-Stars). The *starting lineups* for each team are selected by a vote of the fans. The rest of the players on each team are selected by the NHL's Hockey Operations Department which consults with a committee of senior general managers. This committee tries to select at least one representative from each NHL team, but as the number of teams in the NHL has grown through expansion, this has become more difficult to do.

The first unofficial All-Star game was played in Toronto, in February 1934, following an unfortunate incident. In 1933, *Eddie Shore*, the most feared *defenseman* in hockey, became frustrated by his opponents' incredible stickhandling which denied his Boston Bruins the *puck* during a *power play* opportunity. On one play, after he was mercilessly thrown to the ground, he rose up and skated full force into an innocent *Ace Bailey*, flipping him over his shoulder. Bailey hovered between life and death with a serious head injury. He recovered, but never played hockey again. The game in 1934 was intended as a benefit for Bailey; Shore was booed on center ice until Bailey embraced him in forgiveness.

The first official All-Star Game was also played in Toronto, hosted by the Toronto Maple Leafs in 1947. Until 1968 (except for two seasons), the *Stanley Cup* defending champion hosted the All-Star Game, playing against the selected team of All-Stars. Beginning in 1969, the game was played between representatives of the league's two *conferences*. For the first 19 years, the game was played before the start of the regular season, shifting to mid-season in 1967. In 1979 and 1987, the NHL All-Star team broke from its usual interconference format and played opposite a team from the Soviet Union. No game was held in 1995 due to a work stoppage, and in 1998, the first All-Star battle was held between players from North America and those from the rest of the world.

In 2002 the NHL began playing a "Young Guns" game on the Friday of All-Star weekend, an annual *4-on-4* exhibition game featuring the league's top young players. The league selects 24 players age 25 and younger to compete in this game.

ALL-STAR TEAMS
To clarify a point of frequent confusion, it is different for a player to play in the All-Star Game than it is for a player to be selected to the *All-Star Team*. The players who participate in the All-Star Game are chosen a month before the mid-season point by the fans and a committee of general managers. The players who are selected to the All-Star Team are chosen at the end of each season by the *Professional Hockey Writers' Association*; they do not play a game. For the All-Star Team, 12 players are selected, 2 representatives for each of the 6 player positions (First-Team All-Stars and Second-Team All-Stars). They are chosen because they have excelled in their particular position during the season.

THE HOCKEY HALL OF FAME

The *Hockey Hall of Fame* was founded in 1943 in Toronto, Ontario, Canada. It first opened to the public on August 26, 1961 with a $500,000 facility built in the city's Exhibition Park. A new center opened on June 18, 1993 on the corner of Yonge and Front Streets in downtown Toronto. Those honored are selected annually by hockey experts on a selection committee that includes former players and coaches, and induction into the Hall takes place each November. It generally takes 3 years after retirement for a player or referee to be eligible for membership, but this period can be shortened in exceptional cases as determined by the Hockey Hall of Fame Board of Directors. Inductees are in one of three categories: players, *referees* and builders. The builders group includes team owners, executives from professional and amateur leagues and clubs, and other non-players who have distinguished themselves through their help in the development and promotion of the sport.

The *United States Hockey Hall of Fame*, located in Eveleth, Minnesota, opened in June 1973 to honor notable American players and pay tribute to hockey's innovators. A committee selects new members each year from among players, *coaches*, referees and administrators to be inducted in October.

NHL HOCKEY TROPHIES

HART MEMORIAL TROPHY: Awarded to the *NHL's* Most Valuable Player as selected by a vote of the *Professional Hockey Writers' Association* at the end of the *regular season.* The original Hart Trophy was donated in 1923 by Dr. David A. Hart, father of Cecil Hart, former manager-coach of the *Montreal Canadiens.* The award was presented to the NHL in 1960 after the original Hart Trophy was retired to the *Hockey Hall of Fame. Wayne Gretzky* won this award with the Edmonton Oilers and Los Angeles Kings 9 times.

ART ROSS TROPHY: Awarded to the player who leads the NHL in *points* scored during the regular season. Ties for the lead are decided by giving the trophy first to the player with the most *goals,* then to the one with the fewer number of games played, then to the player who scored his first goal of the season at the earlier date. The trophy was presented to the NHL in 1947 by Art Ross, the former manager-coach of the Boston Bruins. Won by Wayne Gretzky 10 times, *Gordie Howe* of Detroit and *Mario Lemieux* of Pittsburgh each 6 times, *Phil Esposito* of Boston and *Jaromir Jagr* of Pittsburgh each 5 times, and *Stan Mikita* of Chicago 4 times.

MAURICE "ROCKET" RICHARD AWARD: Awarded to the NHL's top *goal*-scorer during the regular season. First granted in 1998-99, this award is named in honor of *Maurice "Rocket" Richard,* the first player ever to score 50 goals in a season.

JAMES NORRIS MEMORIAL TROPHY: Awarded to the league's best *defenseman* as selected by a vote of the Professional Hockey Writers' Association at the end of the regular season. Presented in 1953 in honor of the late owner-president of the Detroit Red Wings by his four children. Won by *Bobby Orr* of Boston 8 times, *Doug Harvey* of Montreal 7 times and *Ray Bourque* of Boston 5 times.

VEZINA TROPHY: Awarded to the *goalie* voted most valuable by NHL team general managers. Until the 1981-82 season, the trophy was awarded to the goalie for the team which had the fewest goals scored against it during the regular season. The trophy was presented to the NHL in 1926-27 by the owners of the Montreal Canadiens in memory of *Georges Vezina*, an outstanding former Canadien goalkeeper. Won by *Jacques Plante* of Montreal and St. Louis 7 times, Bill Durnan of Montreal and *Dominik Hasek* of Buffalo each 6 times, and *Terry Sawchuk* of Detroit and Toronto 4 times.

CALDER MEMORIAL TROPHY: Awarded to the league's outstanding *rookie*, "the player selected as the most proficient in his first year of competition" in the NHL. Selected by a vote of the Professional Hockey Writers' Association at the end of the regular season. Originated in 1937 by *Frank Calder*, the first NHL *President*. After his death in 1943, the NHL presented the *Calder Memorial Trophy* in his memory. Players who are older than 26 prior to the start of the season, or that participated in more than 25 games in any preceding season or in six or more games in each of any two preceding seasons are not eligible. Top rookies were named but no trophy was presented from 1932-1937.

CONN SMYTHE TROPHY: Awarded to the *Most Valuable Player* in the *Stanley Cup playoffs* as selected by a vote of the Professional Hockey Writers' Association at the end of the *Stanley Cup finals*. The trophy was presented by Maple Leaf Gardens, Ltd. in 1964 to honor the Toronto Maple Leafs' former coach, manager, president and owner-governor. The first 29 trophies awarded went to Canadian players. The first time an American was honored was in 1994 when Brian Leetch of the New York Rangers won it.

LADY BYNG TROPHY: Awarded to the player combining the best type of sportsmanship and gentlemanly conduct plus a high standard of playing ability. Selected by a vote of the Professional Hockey Writers' Association at the end of the regular season. Lady Byng, wife of the then Governor-General of Canada, presented the trophy to the NHL in 1925. Frank Boucher of the New York Rangers was given the original award to keep after winning it 7 times in 8 seasons. Lady Byng donated another trophy in 1936.

BILL MASTERTON TROPHY: Awarded by the Professional Hockey Writers' Association to "the NHL player who exemplifies the qualities of perseverance, sportsmanship and dedication to hockey." Presented in 1968 by the NHL Writers' Association in memory of the Minnesota North Star player who died that year from an injury sustained in a hockey game.

KING CLANCY MEMORIAL TROPHY: Awarded "to the player who best exemplifies leadership qualities on and off the ice and has made a noteworthy humanitarian contribution in his community." It was presented by the NHL's Board of Governors in 1988 in memory of Frank "King" Clancy of the Toronto Maple Leafs, honoring his service as a player, coach, *referee* and executive.

WILLIAM M. JENNINGS AWARD: Awarded to the goalie(s) on the team which gives up the fewest goals during the regular season. A goalie must play at least 25 games to be eligible. The trophy was presented to the NHL in 1982 by the NHL's Board of Governors in memory of William M. Jennings, who was instrumental in the league's *expansion* from six teams to 21. Multiple recipients from the same team are possible each year.

FRANK J. SELKE AWARD: Awarded to the *forward* "who best excels in the defensive aspects of the game," as selected by a vote of the Professional Hockey Writers' Association at the end of the regular season. The trophy was presented to the NHL in 1977 by the NHL's Board of Governors in honor of Frank J. Selke, who spent more than 60 years in the game as a coach, manager and front-office executive.

LESTER B. PEARSON AWARD: Awarded to the NHL's outstanding player of the year as selected by a vote of the *NHL's Players' Association (NHLPA)*. It was presented by the NHLPA in 1970-71 in honor of the late Prime Minister of Canada. Won by Wayne Gretzky of Edmonton 5 times, Mario Lemieux of Pittsburgh 4 times and *Guy Lafleur* of Montreal 3 times.

PLUS/MINUS AWARD: This annual award goes to the player who, after playing a minimum of 60 games, leads the NHL in the *plus/minus* statistic at the end of the regular season. A plus/minus award has been presented since 1982-83.

JACK ADAMS AWARD: Awarded since 1974 by the NHL Broadcasters' Association to the "NHL *coach* adjudged to have contributed the most to his team's success." It is presented in the memory of the longtime coach and general manager of the Detroit Red Wings.

LESTER PATRICK TROPHY: Awarded for outstanding service to hockey in the U.S. as selected by a rotating 8-member committee of individuals involved with the sport. Eligible recipients are players, *officials*, coaches, executives and referees. Presented by the New York Rangers in 1966 to honor the memory of its long-time general manager and coach. There can be multiple winners each year.

PRESIDENT'S TROPHY: Awarded annually by the President of the NHL to the club finishing the regular season with the best overall record. It was presented by the NHL Board of Governors to the NHL in 1985-86.

PRINCE OF WALES TROPHY: Since 1981-82, this trophy has gone to the winner of the *Wales Conference* (which was renamed the *Eastern Conference* starting with the 1993-94 season) who advances to the Stanley Cup finals. The Prince of Wales donated the trophy to the NHL in 1924. From 1927-1938, it was presented to the team finishing first in the American Division of the NHL. From 1938-1967, it was given to the first-place team in the one-division league. From 1968-1981 it was awarded to the first-place finisher in the East Division which was renamed the Wales Conference in 1974, and from 1981-93 it was given to the playoff champion in the Wales Conference. Since 1993-94 it has gone to the Eastern Conference champion.

CLARENCE S. CAMPBELL BOWL: Named for the former President of the NHL, this award originally was given to the champions of the West Division. Since 1974-75, it has gone to the team advancing to the Stanley Cup finals as the winner of the *Campbell Conference*, which was renamed the *Western Conference* starting with the 1993-94 season.

HOCKEY PERSONALITIES: PAST AND PRESENT

In this section you will find short biographies on some of the most famous hockey players of the past as well as current stars; also included are the NHL's *Presidents* and *Commissioner*. Although there have been many great players over the years, limited space prevents us from listing them all. Please do not be disappointed if some of your favorites are not here. All statistics in this section are current through the end of the 2001-02 *regular season*. The following key of abbreviations applies to the entries that follow:

A = active player
All-Star Game = a mid-season exhibition game between NHL players selected by fan ballots and team general managers
All-Star Team = the best 2 NHL players at each position (6 on a "First Team", 6 on a "Second Team") selected each year by pro hockey writers
Art Ross Trophy = scoring champion
Calder Trophy = Rookie of the Year
Conn Smythe = Playoff MVP
D = defenseman

F = forward
G = goalie
HF = inducted into Hall of Fame
Lady Byng Trophy = for sportsmanship
MVP = Most Valuable Player
Norris Trophy = best defenseman
R = retired
Top 50 = The Hockey News' Top 50 NHL players of all-time (1997)
Vezina Trophy = best goalie
WHA = World Hockey Association

AMONTE, TONY (F, A) One of a growing number of players to join the NHL by way of the U.S. college system, Amonte played 3 seasons with the New York Rangers before joining the Chicago Blackhawks in 1994. With his intelligence, incredible speed and ability to shoot the puck, this *right wing* is a constant scoring threat, especially on *power plays*. A natural *goal* scorer with a leader's mentality, he was named team *captain* in 2000. Amonte scored 30+ goals in 7 of his first 9 NHL seasons and played in 5 consecutive *All-Star Games* (1997-2001). He scored the game-winning goal for the U.S. in the deciding game of the 1996 World Cup and was selected as a member of the 2002 U.S. Olympic Team. Amonte enjoys golfing, volleyball, and competing against his son Ty in video games.

BELFOUR, ED (G, A): The "Eagle" is an aggressive *goaltender* who often uses his body to stop the puck and possesses great instincts and reflexes that allow him to frequently leave the *crease*. He started his NHL career with the Chicago Blackhawks in 1991 by winning the *Calder Trophy* as *Rookie*-of-the-Year, the *Vezina Trophy* and the *Jennings*

Award for the best *goals-against average* in the league. He won the Vezina again in 1992, either won or shared the Jennings 3 more times (1993, 1995, 1999) and led the Dallas Stars to a *Stanley Cup* championship in 1999. Eddie also played in 5 *All-Star Games.* In addition to enjoying scuba diving, fishing, golf and drag racing, Eddie flies his own plane and is a passionate collector of classic muscle cars from the late '60s and early '70s. He is also active with the Make-a-Wish Foundation.

BELIVEAU, JEAN: (F, HF, Top 50) When he refused to give up his amateur status (and the $20,000 salary that it brought him), the *Montreal Canadiens* purchased the entire Quebec Senior League and turned it from an amateur into a professional league. This left him no choice but to join Montreal in 1953, where he went on to become the then-highest scoring center in NHL history with 1,219 points and 507 goals in 18 seasons. During his career he went to the playoffs 17 times (16 consecutive) and played on 10 *Stanley Cup* championship teams (his name also was added to the Cup 7 more times as an executive). Beliveau was selected playoff *MVP* in 1965; he was also selected to the *All-Star Team* 10 times and won the *Hart Trophy* twice.

BETTMAN, GARY: (Commissioner, A) He was selected as the first *Commissioner* of the NHL in February 1993, replacing interim President Gil Stein. As the Senior Vice-President and General Counsel of the National Basketball Association he had successfully marketed the sport of basketball internationally. In his first year with the NHL, Bettman made good his promise to bring the league into the mainstream of American sports by landing the NHL's first network television deal (a 5-year $155 million contract with Fox Network) and several major sponsors (including Anheuser-Busch Cos. and Nike, Inc.). Early in his tenure Bettman knew little about hockey and was accused of pursuing overall league profits at the expense of small market teams. However, his tough negotiating skills have helped him over the years in labor disputes with on-ice *officials* and players.

BLAKE, ROB (D, A): A physical defenseman who anticipates plays well and also contributes on offense, he made his NHL debut with the Los Angeles Kings in 1989. In each of his first 4 years with the team, "Blakey" was named their Most Outstanding Defenseman and soon received league recognition with the *Norris Trophy* (1998), 4 *All-Star Games* (1994, 1999, 2000, 2001), and 2 *All-Star Team* honors (2000, 2001). Following 12 seasons with the Kings, he was traded to the Colorado Avalanche where immediately he was instrumental in their winning the Stanley Cup (2001). Blakey has also represented Canada in five World Championships (1991, 1994, 1997, 1998, 1999), the 1998

Olympics and the 1996 World Cup of Hockey. His favorite sport after hockey is volleyball, and if he were not a hockey player he would be a farmer. Blake recently launched a clothing line, called Blueline, which targets 11-25 year-olds interested in extreme sports. He is married and has one child, two dogs (a Great Dane and a Pug), two turtles and fish.

BOSSY, MIKE: (F, HF, Top 50) His 10-year career shortened by back problems, Bossy started quickly by winning the *Calder Trophy* (1977-78) and setting a record for most *goals* by a *rookie* (67), not broken until 1992-93 by *Teemu Selanne*. Despite smoking 2 packs of cigarettes a day, he averaged 61 goals and 116 *points* a season his first 6 years, on his way to accumulating 573 career goals and 8 *All-Star Team* selections. The "Boss" set a *right wing* record in 1981-82 by scoring 147 points (64 goals, 83 *assists*, 80-game season), which stood until *Jaromir Jagr* broke it in 1995-96 (in an 82-game season). Bossy would have won the scoring trophy that year but for *Wayne Gretzky*'s record-breaking 212 points and 92 goals. A gentleman who found violence repulsive and refused to fight, Bossy was awarded his first of 3 *Lady Byng Trophies* the following year. An instrumental force in the New York Islanders' 4 consecutive *Stanley Cup* championships (1981-1984), Bossy scored the series-winning goal in both 1982 and 1983 (the only player ever to do so in consecutive years), won the *Conn Smythe* award in 1982 and scored a record 17 *playoff* goals the next year. He set records by scoring 50+ goals in 9 consecutive seasons and 60+ in 5 seasons (both now shared with Gretzky). Since retiring at age 29 he rarely skates due to back pain. Back at home, he became a beloved Quebec Nordiques announcer and then until 1996 was Quebec's #1 morning radio personality.

BOURQUE, RAY: (D, R) An institution with the Boston Bruins where he played for 21 straight years (1979-00), Bourque won the *Stanley Cup* only after being traded to the Colorado Avalanche in his final season (2001). Named *Rookie of the Year* (*Calder Trophy*) in 1979-80, this perennial *All-Star* (a record 19 consecutive appearances) won the *Norris Trophy* for best *defenseman* an impressive 5 times (1986-87, 1987-88, 1989-90, 1990-91, 1993-94). Serving as captain or co-captain of the Bruins since 1985, Bourque was honored for his leadership with a *King Clancy Memorial Trophy* in 1991-92. When he won the Stanley Cup, so respected was Bourque's contribution that Colorado *captain Joe Sakic* departed from tradition by immediately handing the Cup to him to carry for the victory skate. Known for speed and agility, Bourque retired as the leading NHL defenseman in *points* (1,579), *assists* (1,169 – 3rd among all players) and *goals* (410), and is 3rd among all players in games played (1,612).

BOWMAN, SCOTTY: (Coach, HF, R) The most successful *coach* in *NHL* history, Bowman has won more games than any other coach (1,193) and more *playoff* games (207) than any coach in the history of major team sports. Bowman got an early start, coaching a junior team of 20-year-olds when he was just 21. In his 26-year career, 3 different NHL teams he coached won 9 *Stanley Cups* in 13 finals appearances. With Bowman at the helm, the *Montreal Canadiens* won 5 Cups including 4 straight (1976-79), and the Pittsburgh Penguins won in 1991 and 1992. To add to his incredible career, he coached the Detroit Red Wings to 2 straight Stanley Cups in 1997 and 1998, their first in 42 years, and a third in 2002, retiring as a champion shortly thereafter. These teams all had one thing in common: Bowman the master motivator in charge, driving his players hard and emphasizing teamwork. He is one of the first coaches to use videotape and exploit individual *matchups* on the ice.

BRODEUR, MARTIN: (G, A) This son of an Olympic bronze medallist *goalie*/photographer for the *Montreal Canadiens* started his hockey career by playing *forward* and accompanying his dad to games where he idolized *Patrick Roy*. When given a choice to switch to goalie by his *coach*, Martin made the most important decision of his life at the age of 7! As an NHL *rookie* he won the *Calder Memorial Trophy* (1994) and went on to win the *Jennings Trophy* twice (1997, 1998), appeared in 5 consecutive *All-Star Games* (1996-00) and was named to the *All-Star Team* twice (1997, 1998). Brodeur set an NHL record with 43 wins in 1997-98 (a feat he repeated in 1999-00) and his stingy goaltending for the New Jersey Devils was instrumental in helping them win 2 *Stanley Cups* (1995, 2000). He was also a member of Canada's gold medal Olympic team in 2002. Known for his outstanding play outside the *net*, Brodeur is considered one of the best puck-handling goalies in the NHL today, if not ever. Consistency and endurance have been hallmarks of his stellar career. Incredibly, Brodeur's best years might still be ahead of him — in 2001, he became the youngest NHL goalie to record his 300th *regular-season* win. He wears the names of his 3 sons (including twins) on the back of his mask.

BURE, PAVEL: (F, A) Dubbed the "Russian Rocket" because of his blazing speed on the ice, Bure is one of the most explosive scorers in professional hockey. As a teenage rising star in the Soviet Union, he helped the national team win a world hockey *title* before defecting to North America in 1991, signing with the NHL's Vancouver Canucks. He quickly established himself in his first season, scoring 34 *goals* in only 65 games on his way to winning the *Calder Trophy* and then scoring 60 goals in each of his first 2 full seasons. In all, he has led the NHL in goals 4 times (1993-94,

1997-98, 1999-00, 2000-01) and led Russia to the silver medal as the leading scorer in the 1998 Olympics (9 goals). When traded to the Florida Panthers in 1998, this *right wing* continued to impress but over the next few years was also plagued by injuries. In March 2002, the team opted to trade him to the N.Y. Rangers rather than re-sign him to a $10M contract. Pavel's brother Valeri Bure is a right wing for the Calgary Flames. Pavel provided tabloid fodder in 2000 following his surprise engagement after a 4-month courtship to Russian tennis superstar/model Anna Kournikova, 10 years his junior, despite her decade-long romantic ties to Bure's ex-teammate *Sergei Federov* (whom she is rumored to have secretly married in 2001).

COFFEY, PAUL: (D, R, Top 50) One of the NHL's swiftest skaters known for his end-to-end rushes, this goal-scoring *defenseman* joined the NHL in 1980 and was a key member of the 3-time *Stanley Cup* champion Edmonton Oilers (1983-84, 1985-86 and 1986-87). Over his 21-year career this 13-time *All-Star* compiled impressive offensive numbers for a defensemen, including 396 *goals* and 1,135 *assists* (both 2nd-most to *Ray Borque)*, the longest scoring streak (28 games, 1985-86) and the most goals in a single season (48, 1985-86). Coffey even silenced critics of his defensive abilities by winning 3 *Norris Trophies* (1984-85, 1985-86 and 1994-95). A 1987 trade brought him to the Pittsburgh Penguins where he helped them win their first Stanley Cup. Before retiring in 2001, Coffey played with 6 more teams. Today he is involved with the Make-A-Wish Foundation.

DIONNE, MARCEL: (F, HF, Top 50) The incredible 18-year career of this gifted, consistent *center* and prolific *goal* scorer was somewhat overlooked in the obscure Los Angeles hockey market. With his games rarely televised, few witnessed his accomplishments in becoming the NHL's third all-time leading goal scorer (731, behind only *Wayne Gretzky* and *Gordie Howe*) and fourth all-time leading scorer (1,771 *points*). Even as an exceptionally talented amateur, Dionne's abilities were eclipsed by rival Canadian *Guy Lafleur* who was selected 1st in the 1971 *draft*, leaving Dionne for the Detroit Red Wings' #2 pick. Four years later Dionne was traded to the L.A. Kings, where he led the efficient "Triple Crown" line (with Dave Taylor and Charlie Simmer), one of the highest-scoring trios in NHL history. He was the first player to score 100 points in each of 8 seasons, won the *Art Ross Trophy* (1979-80), won the *Lady Byng Trophy* twice (1975 and 1977), and was an 8-time *All-Star*. The Kings (who have retired his #16 jersey) traded him to the N.Y. Rangers during the 1986-87 season. This popular and outgoing legend retired in 1989. He lives in Toronto and believes today's players "have lost that personal touch with the fans" which marked his era.

DRYDEN, KEN: (G, HF, Top 50) Often referred to as a human octopus, this unusually tall *goalie* (6'4") played only 8 seasons but was the backbone of the *Montreal Canadiens* in winning 6 *Stanley Cup* championships (4 consecutive) during the 1970s. Despite only playing 6 regular-season games in 1971 (simultaneously completing his law degree), he won the *Conn Smythe Trophy* as *playoff MVP*, and then won the *Calder Trophy* in his *rookie* season (1971-72). This 5-time *All-Star* won or shared the *Vezina Trophy* for best goalie 5 times and led the league in *shutouts* 4 times, ending his short 397-game career with 46 shutouts and a near-record 2.24 *goals-against average*. Surprisingly, Dryden retired at age 31 at the height of his career to work as a $7,000-a-year law clerk, moved to England where he wrote 2 hockey books, and then returned to Toronto in 1982 to practice law.

ESPOSITO, PHIL: (F, HF, Top 50) "Espo" retired in January 1981 after 18 seasons as the then-second highest scorer in NHL history after *Gordie Howe* with 1,590 *points* (717 *goals* and 873 *assists*). He was the first player to score over 100 points in a season (126 in 1968-69) and he surpassed 55 goals a season 5 consecutive times. Surprisingly Espo did not show an interest in playing hockey until he was a teenager and was plagued by weight problems that almost kept him out of the NHL. His NHL career began with the Chicago Blackhawks, but in 1967 he was traded to the Boston Bruins where he spent 8½ seasons. He sparked the Bruins to two *Stanley Cup* championships in 1970 and 1972, the team's first in 29 years. His greatest season came in 1970-71 when he established new single-season records for goals (76) and points (152), both of which stood a full decade before they were broken by *Wayne Gretzky*. Esposito won the *Art Ross Trophy* 5 times and the *Hart Trophy* twice. In 1975 he was traded to the New York Rangers, where he rarely played up to his old Boston form. He retired in 1981, ending a career that included being selected to the *All-Star Team* 10 times. After a few brief stints as coach and general manager of the New York Rangers in the late 1980s, in 1992 he became part-owner and the first general manager of the Tampa Bay Lightning *expansion team*. Now retired, this avid golfer is working on his own TV show and a book on hockey. His brother Tony was one of the NHL's greatest *goalies*.

ESPOSITO, TONY: (G, HF) He made a brief appearance with the *Montreal Canadiens* before being signed to the Chicago Blackhawks in 1969, where he revolutionized goaltending with his legs-open *butterfly style* and dramatic on-ice flops. His first full season (1969-70) was one of the best ever by a goalie, as he won the *Calder Trophy*, the

Vezina Trophy for best *goalie* with his 2.17 *goals-against average*, was named to the *All-Star Team* and established a modern-day NHL record with 15 *shutouts* which still stands today. He shared the Vezina Trophy 2 more times, was an All-Star 4 more times and helped Chicago win 9 *division titles* (including 4 consecutive). He retired in 1984 as the then-oldest NHL player at age 40 with 76 career shutouts, a modern-day *goalie* record. He then joined the executive ranks, first with the Pittsburgh Penguins and then with older brother Phil in Tampa Bay, ultimately retiring in Florida.

FORSBERG, PETER: (F, A) This Swedish League Player of the Year (1993-94) was selected 6th overall by the Philadelphia Flyers and traded to the Quebec Nordiques (now the Colorado Avalanche), where he became an instrumental force in that team winning 4 straight *division titles* and its first *Stanley Cup* (1996). A smooth skater with explosive speed, he controls the puck well and is an outstanding playmaker who still relishes contact. In his *rookie* year, Forsberg won the *Calder Memorial Trophy* (1994-95), and has since been named an *All-Star* 4 times. After he scored the winning goal that earned Sweden the gold medal in the 1994 Olympics, Forsberg became the first hockey player honored on a Swedish postage stamp. Unfortunately, Forsberg has suffered several injuries, the most recent of which required the removal of his spleen during the 2001 *playoffs*. Afterwards he shocked the hockey world when he announced he was taking a year off to rest, heal and rethink whether he would return to the NHL. Despite missing the entire 2002 regular season, Forsberg returned to become the NHL's leading scorer in the playoffs.

GARTNER, MIKE: (F, HF) Despite the fact that Gartner's 19-year NHL career took him from the Washington Capitals to the Minnesota North Stars to the New York Rangers to the Toronto Maple Leafs to the *expansion* Phoenix Coyotes, his ability to score consistently remained unaffected. Gartner was a finesse player, known for his remarkable speed, flawless technical form and durability (this 38-year old did not miss a single game his last 2 seasons). He holds the NHL career record for most consecutive 30-*goal* seasons (15 from 1979-80 to 1993-94, a streak broken only by the NHL labor trouble) and the most 30+ goal seasons (17), and is 5th all-time in goals scored (708). This 7-time *All-Star* was also named All-Star *MVP* in 1993 and shares an All-Star Game record for most goals scored (4 in 1991). Gartner is a born-again Christian who coaches kids in Toronto.

GRETZKY, WAYNE: (F, HF, Top 50) Aptly nicknamed "The Great One", Gretzky is generally regarded as the best hockey player of all time. He began skating in a makeshift backyard rink at the age of 3, took the amateur leagues by storm and went on to rewrite the *NHL* record books during his 21-year tenure. His first pro contract with the *WHA* was signed at age 17 for $1.7 million (1978). Eight games later he was sold to the Edmonton Oilers, signing a 21-year contract for $5 million, but in 1982 he renegotiated, receiving over $1 million a year to become the then-highest paid player in NHL history. Gretzky was well worth it.

Wayne Gretzky.

In each of his first 8 seasons he won the *Hart Trophy* as league MVP (the 1st-ever rookie MVP) and earned the *Art Ross Trophy* in each of his first 7 seasons (10 career). His 3rd season he eclipsed *Phil Esposito*'s previously untouchable *goal*-scoring record to finish with an astounding 92 goals, 120 *assists* and 212 points, all single-season records. He later broke his own season record for points, setting the current standard at 215; the goals record still stands at 92, and the only player to break the single-season assists record has been Gretzky himself, 5 different times. With such an audacious start, it is no surprise that Gretzky's name appears beside nearly every NHL record that relates to scoring, for both the *regular season* and *playoffs* or that he played in the *All-Star Game* every season. His career total of 2,857 points appears untouchable (next-best is only 1,804). On March 23, 1994, Gretzky reached one of the only milestones left when he scored his 802nd career goal to break *Gordie Howe*'s record, a feat he accomplished in 15 years compared to Howe's 26. Focusing on Gretzky's individual accomplishments ignores that he was the consummate team player, *captaining* the Oilers to 4 *Stanley Cups* during the 1980s, receiving the *Conn Smythe Trophy* twice (1985, 1988). Even though Gretzky was surrounded by extraordinary talent in teammates like *Mark Messier, Jari Kurri* and *Paul Coffey*, it was his playmaking ability that took them to the highest levels. With Gretzky's perfect passes, sometimes even setting up his *defensemen*, his teammates frequently caught opponents by surprise.

In 1988, the same year he married actress Janet Jones, he was traded to the Los Angeles Kings where he promptly earned his 9th Hart Trophy and then spent 8 years setting and breaking more records. After part of a year with the St. Louis Blues, he joined the New York Rangers as a *free agent* in 1996, ultimately retiring in 1999. His #99 (adopted because his favorite #9 was taken when he joined an amateur team in 1977) was immediately retired league-wide and the *Hall of Fame* waived its waiting period, inducting him without delay. This classy, dignified and articulate legend is a role model (he won the *Lady Byng Trophy* 5 times), a true ambassador for hockey and a spokesperson for family-oriented and wholesome products. However, these same traits made certain endorsements more elusive as some did not consider him "tough" enough to be associated with hockey. Though he has lived in the U.S. since 1988, he has remained committed to his roots by representing Canada in international competition, leading to his being honored in 2002 with the highest Olympic award, the Olympic Order. Today, Gretzky is part-owner of the Phoenix Coyotes and a spokesman for the fight against arthritis.

HALL, GLENN: (G, HF, Top 50) "Mr. Goalie" started his NHL career with the Detroit Red Wings by winning the *Calder Trophy* in 1955-56. He went on to win the *Vezina Trophy* 3 times and was selected to the *All-Star Team* in 11 of his 14 seasons in the NHL. Hall led the NHL in *shutouts* for 6 seasons and still holds the record for the most consecutive complete games by a goaltender (502), ending his career in 1971 with an excellent 2.51 *goals-against average*. Hall's longevity is even more remarkable considering he disliked being a goalie and got sick before each game (some joke his bucket should be in the *Hall of Fame*), staying only to support his family. He was traded to Chicago in his third season where in 1961, he helped the Blackhawks win their first *Stanley Cup* in 23 years by holding a *Montreal Canadiens* team that included *Jean Beliveau*, *Rocket Richard* and "Boom Boom" Geoffrion scoreless for 135 minutes and 26 seconds. In 1968, he led his third team, the expansion St. Louis Blues, into the first of 3 consecutive Stanley Cup finals where, despite their loss in 4 straight games, he still emerged as the *playoff MVP* winning the *Conn Smythe Trophy*. Until the second half of his final season, Hall played without a mask yet did not miss one minute of play in 7 years (1955-1962) at a time when NHL teams carried only one goalie. After retiring, Hall was a goaltending coach for several NHL teams.

HARVEY, DOUG: (D, HF, Top 50) This all-around athlete (baseball and football) was a 7-time winner of the *James Norris Trophy* as the NHL's leading *defenseman* and named to the *All-Star Team* 11 times in his 17 seasons with the NHL that began in 1947. He played the *point* on the *Montreal Canadiens'* awesome *power play* during the 1950s that could score numerous *goals* against *shorthanded* teams; this was the team that caused the NHL to change its rules and permit a player penalized by a *minor penalty* to return to the ice as soon as a single goal is scored against his team. With the Canadiens he won 6 *Stanley Cups* (5 consecutive). In 1961 he was traded to the New York Rangers and, after a stint in the minors, finished his NHL career with the St. Louis Blues in 1969 by helping them reach the Stanley Cup finals. Blacklisted by the NHL for being involved in the first attempt to form a players' union, Harvey's number was not retired by the Canadiens until 1985. He died in 1989 at the age of 65.

HASEK, DOMINIK: (G, R) A top NHL *goalie* in the 1990s with the Buffalo Sabres, Hasek asked to be traded after 9 seasons so he could have a chance at winning a *Stanley Cup*. In only his first year with the Detroit Red Wings (2002), he did exactly that, recording a *playoff* record 6 *shutouts* in clinching victory. His dream finally fulfilled, Hasek promptly retired from hockey. Hasek's unorthodox style (he flopped like a fish, flailed, sprawled, abandoned his *stick* and relied on his terrific leg reflexes to stop the *puck*!) did not stop "the Dominator" from being considered among the world's best goalies (an opinion espoused by none other than *Wayne Gretzky*).

This son of a uranium miner began playing goal as a toddler, his first pair of skates a pair of shoes with blades screwed into the soles. Despite lucrative offers from the Chicago Blackhawks who *drafted* him in 1983, Hasek did not join the NHL until 7 years later, preferring the perks of being the top goalie in hockey-crazed Czechoslovakia. With a trade to the Buffalo Sabres in 1992 he finally proved his worth. He was consistently at the top of the NHL in *save percentage*, leading the league for 6 consecutive seasons starting in 1993-94 while winning the *Vezina Trophy* 6 times in 8 years. Hasek also won the *Hart Memorial Trophy* twice (quite an accomplishment for any player, let alone a goalie). In 1998, Hasek added an Olympic gold medal to his accomplishments, playing an instrumental role that included 20 *saves* in the victory game for his homeland; he was honored by Czech astronomers who named an asteroid after him. Hasek, who resembles Kraemer on Seinfeld, has behaved erratically in recent years when he felt wronged, including emotional outbursts, going after a player on the ice and grabbing a reporter (which cost him a 3-*playoff* game suspension and $10,000 fine). His notorious temper notwithstanding, he is gentle with children and the founder of a hockey program for needy youngsters.

HOWE, GORDIE: (F, HF, Top 50) The ambidextrous "Mr. Hockey" actually kept a scrapbook his first year in the NHL expecting to need proof of his ever having played there. Instead he became the most enduring player in the history of professional hockey, having played 32 seasons (26 with the NHL, 6 with the *World Hockey Association (WHA)*) before retiring in 1980 (for the second and final time) at the age of 52. Howe established many NHL records, some of which he still retains. At the time he retired, he held the all-time records

Gordie Howe.

for *goals* (801), *assists* (1,049) and *points* (1,850), and today he remains second only to *Wayne Gretzky* in goals and points (his goal record stood for 31 years until 1994). He won the *Art Ross Trophy* 6 times (including 4 consecutive seasons) and was a 6-time winner of the *Hart Trophy* as *MVP*. Combining his NHL and WHA statistics, including *playoff* games, Howe played in 2,421 games where he collected 1,071 goals, 1,518 assists, 2,589 points and 2,419 *penalty minutes*.

In his 25 years with the Detroit Red Wings, he won 4 *Stanley Cup* championships and was named to the *All-Star Team* a record 21 times. After sitting out 2 years, he returned in 1973 to play with his sons Marty and Mark in the WHA for 6 more seasons; he then finished with one more year in the NHL with the Hartford Whalers. On October 3, 1997, the nearly 70-year old Howe played a shift for Detroit's *IHL* minor league team, making him the first individual to appear in a professional hockey game for each of 6 consecutive decades (1940s-1990s). During a 1950 Stanley Cup game, Howe collided with an opponent and crashed head-on into the sideboards, suffering a severe brain injury. Although he hung between life and death, the injury left him only with a slight facial tic, which is why his teammates called him "Blinky."

HULL, BOBBY: (F, HF, Top 50) Hull, who started skating at age 3, entered the NHL in 1957 and during his first 15 years helped the ailing Chicago Blackhawks become one of the richest *franchises*. In 1972 he accepted the first $1 million contract in hockey history to jump to the *World Hockey Association (WHA)*, where he played 7 ½ seasons with the Winnipeg Jets. He was traded to the Hartford Whalers late in the 1979-80 season and

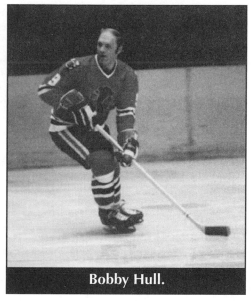

Bobby Hull.

even played a few games with *Gordie Howe* before retiring in 1980 at the age of 41. In his 23-year career Hull amassed 913 *goals* and 1,808 *points* (including his WHA statistics), but only 1 *Stanley Cup* (1961). He was the most dominant scorer of the 1960s and '70s, cracking the 50-goal barrier 5 times with Chicago and 4 more times with the Jets. In 1974-75 he scored a record 77 goals in 78 games. Hull held the NHL record for the most career goals by a *left wing* (610) for over 2 decades until finally surpassed by Luc Robitaille in 2002. He led the NHL in goals scored 7 different seasons, won the *Art Ross Trophy* 3 times, the *Hart Trophy* twice, the *Lady Byng Trophy* once and was selected to the *All-Star Team* 12 times.

Bobby did not, however, become a prolific scorer until his third season when he improved on the *slap shot*, a technique developed by "Boom Boom" Geoffrion of the *Montreal Canadiens* and Andy Bathgate of the New York Rangers, and which became Hull's calling card. Hull also added a curve to the blade of his *stick* which increased the speed of the *puck*. The very high speeds of both his slap shot (118.3 miles per hour, or 35 mph above the league average) and his skating (at almost 30 mph, the fastest in hockey) coupled with his blonde good looks earned him the nickname Golden Jet. Today Hull deals in cattle.

HULL, BRETT: (F, A) This *right wing* followed in father *Bobby Hull*'s skate strides (they are the only father-son combo in NHL history to score 1,000+ *points* and 600+ *goals* each) although he hardly knew him until he was grown (the result of a bitter divorce where Brett went to live with his mother). He developed from a lazy, pudgy kid into one of the most prolific and charismatic hockey players all on his own. Hull is one of the NHL's most feared snipers, appearing from out of nowhere to score. In 17 seasons in the NHL, he amassed 679 goals (6th in league history and 1st among active players) and is also one of only 3 players (with *Wayne Gretzky* and *Mario Lemieux*) to ever score 80+ goals in a single season (86 in 1991-92). He won the *Lady Byng Trophy* (1990) and the *Hart Trophy* (1991), and has been an All-Star 8 times

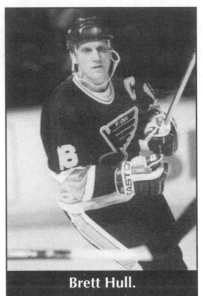

Brett Hull.

to date. The Dallas Stars ended his 10-year stay with the St. Louis Blues by signing him to a 3-year $17.5 million contract in 1998, and he promptly led them to the *Stanley Cup title* his first year there. In 2001 he joined the Detroit Red Wings and also led that team to a Stanley Cup his first year there. Hull is known for his brutal honesty. Though he once claimed he would never marry or have children, he and his wife are the proud parents of 3 kids.

JAGR, JAROMIR: (F, A) Overshadowed by superstar teammate *Mario Lemeiux* for many years, Jagr developed into an offensive force to be reckoned with. The first Czechoslovakian player *drafted* into the NHL without defecting (5th overall in 1990), he quickly played a role in the Pittsburgh Penguins' back-to-back *Stanley Cup* victories (1991, 1992). A powerful skater who is almost impossible to catch, his *wrist shot* is one of the *NHL's* best. The first European-trained player to win the *Art Ross* trophy, he did so 5 times in 7 years (1995, 1998, 1999, 2000, 2001), and won the *Hart Memorial Trophy* in 1999. A member of the Czech team that won the gold medal at the 1998 Olympics, Jagr, once easily recognized for long black hair flowing from his helmet, now sports shorter curls for a new team (Washington Capitols). This team jokester loves dogs and reading science fiction.

KURRI, JARI: (F, HF, Top 50) In his first 10 seasons (1980-90) he was instrumental in helping *Wayne Gretzky* lead the Edmonton Oilers to 4 *Stanley Cup* championships; Kurri and the Oilers won a 5th title without the Great One in 1989-90. He was reunited with

Gretzky on the Los Angeles Kings in 1992, helping also to lead that team into the Stanley Cup finals only to lose to the *Montreal Canadiens* in 1993. He finished his career with the Anaheim Mighty Ducks and Colorado Avalanche. This *goal*-scorer broke the 50-goal barrier 4 consecutive years, which included a 71-goal season in 1984-85, becoming only the third player in history to pass the 70-goal mark after Gretzky and *Phil Esposito*. He is third all-time in *playoff* goals (106) and playoff *points* (233) behind Gretzky and *Mark Messier*, and 5th all-time in playoff *assists* (127). He has won a *Lady Byng Trophy* and has made 8 *All Star Game* appearances. In 1998, Kurri brought home an Olympic bronze medal for his native Finland and retired as the highest-scoring European player in NHL history. Today he is a TV commentator and hockey coach.

LAFLEUR, GUY: (F, HF, Top 50) Nicknamed "The Blond Demon" for his long hair and wild rushes down the ice, this *right wing*'s *goal* scoring led the *Montreal Canadiens* to 4 consecutive *Stanley Cup* championships (1976-1979). He played on the 1976-77 Canadien team that boasts the best single-season record in NHL history, 60-8-12. Lafleur dominated the late 1970s, setting the record for 6 consecutive 50+ goal seasons (which was later broken by *Mike Bossy* in 1983-84) on his way to 3 consecutive *Art Ross Trophies* in 1976, 1977 and 1978. During those years he also picked up 2 *Hart Trophies* (1977 and 1978) and won the *Conn Smythe Trophy* (1977). Lafleur was the youngest to score 400 career goals and achieve 1,000 *points* in the NHL. This 6-time *All-Star* retired in 1984, but 3 years later and after his induction into the *Hall of Fame*, he returned for 3 more seasons before retiring in 1991 for good. Vowing never to leave the sport, he joined the Canadiens front office.

LECLAIR, JOHN: (F, A) At 6'3", 225 lbs., this Philadelphia Flyer is nearly impossible to move away from the *net* where he scrounges for *rebounds* and *deflections* that lead to *goals*. His tactics seem to be working, as he became the first American in NHL history to score 50+ goals in 3 consecutive seasons (1995-1998). His ability to score on the *power play* twice led him to NHL-leading *plus/minus* ratings (+44 in 1996-97, +36 in 1998-99). LeClair, drafted by the *Montreal Canadiens* in 1987, played in relative obscurity except for 2 game-winning *overtime* goals that helped win the *Stanley Cup* in 1993. His play enticed the Philadelphia Flyers to trade for him in 1995, where he became the *left wing* on the "Legion of Doom" line and the team's cornerstone. One of the top U.S.-born players in the NHL (he's from Vermont), LeClair was an integral part of the U.S. team that won the first-ever World Cup in 1996-97. The John LeClair Foundation he started in 1992 hosts golf tournaments which have raised over $750,000 for Vermont children's charities.

LEMIEUX, MARIO: (F, A, HF, Top 50) Lemieux ("the best" in French) has been nothing short of spectacular when healthy, and one can only imagine what he might have done if not besieged by back problems and Hodgkin's disease (a form of cancer). The number one overall *draft pick* in 1984-85 did not disappoint, becoming only the 3rd *rookie* in NHL history to reach 100 *points* and earning the *Calder Trophy*. He started his NHL career by scoring a *goal* on his first shot of his first

Mario Lemieux.

game. He went on to win the *Art Ross Trophy* and the *Hart Trophy* in 1987-88, breaking *Wayne Gretzky's* string of 7 consecutive Art Ross and 8 consecutive Hart Trophies. Lemieux would win the Hart Trophy twice more (1993, 1996) and the Art Ross 5 more times (1989, 1992, 1993, 1996, 1997). He led the Pittsburgh Penguins to their first *Stanley Cup* in 1991, and after an incredible comeback from back surgery, led them to a 2nd *title* in 1992. In both years he was awarded the *Conn Smythe Trophy* for his efforts, becoming only the 2nd player to win it in consecutive seasons. Even after missing 24 games while undergoing radiation treatment for cancer in 1992-93, he sparked his team to an NHL-record 17-game winning streak when he returned to the *lineup* and won his 4th *scoring title* in 6 years. In 1994-95, this superstar decided to sit out the season to recover from lingering fatigue.

He returned with a vengeance in 1995-96, scoring 69 goals and 161 points during the *regular season*, followed by 27 points in 18 *playoff* games in reaching the *Eastern Conference* finals. He was honored with both the Art Ross and Hart Trophies that year. His next season, Lemieux once again led the league with 122 points taking home his 6th Art Ross. When he retired for the first time in 1997, he had been selected to the *All-Star Team* 8 times, led the league in goals 3 times, was twice named Male Athlete of the Year by the

Canadian press (1993, 1998) and accumulated 613 goals, 881 *assists* and 1,494 points in only 745 *regular-season* games, making him the only player to average over 2 points per game in his career (2.01). When the Penguins faced bankruptcy and possible relocation in 1999, Lemieux (himself owed millions in deferred salary) led a group to purchase the team and keep it in Pittsburgh. In 2000, he started another comeback with the Penguins, becoming only the 3rd *Hall of Famer* (along with *Howe* and *Lafleur*) to return to the ice after retirement. Whenever he finally retires, Lemieux will be remembered not just for his leadership and skill, but also for the class with which he presented himself both on and off the ice.

LIDSTROM, NICKLAS: (D, A) Considered perhaps the best all-around *defenseman* in the NHL today, Lidstrom's play is steady, intelligent and subtle rather than physical, fast or flashy. This humble, quiet Swede is unflappable, rarely making a poor *pass*, and his powerful *shots* from the *blue line* often take *goalies* by surprise. As the backbone of the Detroit Red Wings since 1991, Lidstrom thrived under coach *Scotty Bowman*. He was selected to the First *All-Star Team* 4 times (1998-2001), played in 5 *All-Star Games* (1996, 1998-2001), and won 3 *Stanley Cup* championships (1997, 1998, 2002) with the Red Wings, contributing a *Conn Smythe Trophy*-winning performance in the 2002 victory. A perennial runner-up for league wide recognition (he was 2nd in consideration for the *Calder Trophy* his rookie year, for the *Norris* 4 times and the *Lady Byng* twice), Lidstrom finally became the first Swede to win the Norris Trophy, doing it in back-to-back years in 2001 and 2002. In international play, he won gold (1991) and bronze medals (1994) at the World Championships, and was twice named to the Swedish Olympic team (1998, 2002). This popular player (named *captain* of the World Team in the 2000 All-Star Game) is considering a return to Sweden so that his two sons, Kevin and Erik, can be educated there.

MESSIER, MARK: (F, A, Top 50) Renowned for his leadership abilities, the "Moose" is credited with being the most complete player of his generation. An integral member of the powerhouse Edmonton Oiler team that won 4 *Stanley Cups* in the 1980s with *Wayne Gretzky*, Messier took home the *Conn Smythe Trophy* in 1984 and then led the team to a 5th *title* without Gretzky in 1989-90, earning the *Hart Trophy* in the process. Traded to the Rangers in 1991, he immediately won a second Hart Trophy following his 6th 100+ *point* season. During the 1994 *playoffs*, with the Rangers facing elimination against the cross-town rival New Jersey Devils in Game 6, in a feat of legendary proportions, Messier brashly guaranteed a victory and won the game by scoring a *hat trick*. He then scored the winning *goal* in Game 7, leading the Rangers to their first championship in 54 years (his 6th) and becoming the first player to *captain* 2 different teams to Stanley Cup titles. In 1997, he joined the Vancouver Canucks as a *free agent* but in 2000, at age 40, he returned to the Rangers for 3 more years. Messier entered the 2002-03 season as the NHL's active leader in points (1,804, 3rd all-time) and *All-Star Games* (14). Messier's brother, 2 cousins and brother-in-law have all played in the NHL.

MIKITA, STAN: (F, HF, Top 50) This *center* for the Chicago Blackhawks played with *Bobby Hull* and was one of the leading scorers of his era along with Andy Bathgate and *Gordie Howe*. He was selected to the *All-Star Team* 8 times, won the *Art Ross Trophy* 4 times, the *Hart Trophy* twice and the *Lady Byng Trophy* twice. In 1967, he became the first player in NHL history to win all three awards in a single year, a feat he repeated the next year. His claiming of the Lady Byng was surprising considering that he amassed 100+ *penalty* minutes in 4 of his first 7 seasons, but he cleaned up his act after his daughter questioned his style of play, registering only 6 *minor* penalties in 1966-67. In a 22-year career that ended in 1980, he amassed 541 *goals* and 926 *assists* for 1,467 *points* and helped Chicago win the *Stanley Cup* in 1961. In 1972 Mikita founded the American Impaired Hearing Association to help youngsters who are hard of hearing.

Bobby Orr.

ORR, BOBBY: (D, HF, Top 50) Six knee operations cut his brilliant NHL career to 10 years with the Boston Bruins and a few games with the Chicago Blackhawks. When he retired at age 30, Orr held or shared 12 individual NHL records. He was the first player to dish out 100 *assists* (102) in a single season, an incredible feat considering he was a *defenseman*, and to this day he holds the single-season records for most assists (102) and *points* (139) by a defenseman (both set in 1970-71). He started his NHL career in 1967 by winning the *Calder Trophy*, then took home 8 consecutive *Norris Trophies* while revolutionizing the role of defensemen with his slick passing, end-to-end dashes and playmaking. Along the way he scored an astonishing 915 points in 657 games, led the NHL in assists 5 times and is the only defenseman to win the *Art Ross Trophy* — not once, but twice. It was Orr's *overtime goal* that brought the 1970 Bruins their first *Stanley Cup* in 29 years, and he also set 2 *playoff* records (9 goals and 20 points) in that series. That same year, Orr became the first player to win 4 trophies in a single season: the Art Ross, Norris, *Hart* and *Conn Smythe*. He would also become the first player to win the Hart Trophy 3 consecutive years. Named to 8 consecutive *All-Star Teams*, Orr is the youngest player ever elected to the *Hall of Fame* at age 31. In 1971, he was the first player officially represented in contract negotiations by an agent, signing the first $1 million deal in hockey. Today he is one of the game's most powerful agents, recruiting players as young as 14 (the same age at which Boston began recruiting Orr!).

PLANTE, JACQUES: (G, HF, Top 50) In the 10 years he spent with the *Montreal Canadiens*, they won 6 *Stanley Cup* championships (including 5 consecutive *titles* from 1956-1960). He won the *Vezina Trophy* for best *goalie* 7 times (including 5 in a row) and was selected as a member of the *All-Star Team* 7 times. Plante was only the 4th goalie to win the *Hart Trophy* (1962). Over his 21-year career he had an outstanding 2.38 *goals-against average* in 837 games and recorded 82 *shutouts*. In 1959 he was the first goalie to popularize wearing a *face mask*, despite management's opposition, after an injury to his face required stitches, and he pioneered skating behind the *net* to stop *pucks*. When the St. Louis Blues lured him out of retirement in 1968, he promptly won his 7th Vezina Trophy and led that team to two consecutive *division* titles at the age of 40. He then spent 3 seasons with the Toronto Maple Leafs and ended his career in the *World Hockey Association* (WHA) with the Edmonton Oilers in 1974-75. His book, "The Art of Goaltending", was the first of its kind. Plante died in 1986.

POTVIN, DENIS: (D, HF, Top 50) This *goal-scoring defenseman* was the *captain* of the New York Islanders team that won 4 consecutive *Stanley Cup* championships from 1980-1983. This highly-touted first pick of the 1973 *draft* started his 15-year career by winning the *Calder Trophy* (1973-74) and went on to win 3 *Norris Trophies* (1976, 1978 and 1979). Potvin broke several of *Bobby Orr*'s NHL records for defensemen in 1985-86 (915 career *points* and 271 career *goals*), then broke Brad Park's record for career *assists* (684) in 1986-87, then topped it off by becoming the first defenseman to score 300 goals and 1,000 career points. When he retired at the age of 34, he held the NHL's defensemen records for most goals (310), most assists (742) and most points (1,052). He was also selected to the *All-Star Team* 7 times.

PRESIDENTS: The first *President* of the NHL was hockey player *Frank Calder*; appointed in 1917, he served until his death in 1943. *Red Dutton* took over as President through the war years of 1943-1946. He was succeeded by *Clarence Campbell* who was President from 1946-1977. *John A. Ziegler, Jr.* became the 4th President in 1977. He was a Michigan-born lawyer who played amateur hockey. In October 1992 he stepped down, and *Gil Stein* acted as the interim President of the NHL until the league appointed its first *Commissioner, Gary Bettman,* also a lawyer, in February of 1993.

RICHARD, MAURICE ("ROCKET"): (F, HF, Top 50) This working class boy did not play organized hockey until he was 11, was cursed with weak bones that led to frequent fractures and actually studied to be a machinist. He persevered to become a famed high-scoring *right wing* for the *Montreal Canadiens* whose 544 career *goals* stood as the record until broken by *Gordie Howe.* The ambidextrous Rocket was the 1st player in the NHL to score 50 goals during a season (1944-45) and he remains the only player to achieve that in a 50-game schedule. In 18 seasons, he won 8 *Stanley Cups*, was named to the *All-Star Team* 14 times and played in 13 *All-Star Games.* Known for his short temper and for being at the center of controversy, Richard was issued a multiple-game suspension by NHL *President Campbell* for punching a *linesman* in 1955. This came one week before the end of a season in which he was vying to win the scoring championship and extended into the *Stanley Cup playoffs*, precipitating the infamous Ste. Catherine Street riots in downtown Montreal which caused over $1 million of damage. Voted into the *Hall of Fame* only 9 months after his 1960 retirement, Richard joined the Canadiens' public relations department and ventured into the fuel industry and a fishing line business. In 1998, the 76-year old Richard waged a battle against a rare form of abdominal cancer, the same year the NHL dedicated an annual award given in his honor to the league's top goal scorer. When he succumbed to the cancer in May 2000, the Quebec National Assembly was suspended for a day, he was awarded a state funeral and a mass in his honor was broadcast live throughout Canada.

ROY, PATRICK: (G, A, Top 50) As a *rookie* with the *Montreal Canadiens* in 1985-86, "Saint Patrick" became the youngest *playoff MVP,* winning the *Conn Smythe Trophy* and the *Stanley Cup* championship at age 20. He was a member of 3 more Stanley Cup championship teams — with Montreal in 1993, and then after he insisted on being traded, with the Colorado Avalanche in 1995 and 2001, winning the Conn Smythe twice more to become the first player to win that award 3 times. The NHL's all-time winningest *goalie* with 516 career wins to date, Roy eclipsed *Terry Sawchuk's* previously untouchable mark of 447. He has been selected to the *All-Star Team* seven times, played in 9 *All-Star Games* and won 3 *Vezina Trophies* the years he boasted the NHL's best *goals-against average* (2.47 in 1989, 2.53 in 1990 and 2.36 in 1992). His records include most 30+ win seasons (11), most playoff games (228) and most playoff wins (142) by a goaltender. Roy plays *butterfly style,* stays in the net and gives up few rebounds. A superstitious player, before every game Roy writes the names of his 3 children on his stick, eats the same meal, gets dressed and prepares his *crease* the same way.

SAKIC, JOE: (F, A) Selected by the Quebec Nordiques (now the Colorado Avalanche) as an underage junior in the 1ˢᵗ *round* of the 1987 *draft,* Sakic's career really began to flourish in the 1990s. Long considered one of the league's best playmakers, he has recently become one of the game's best shooters, known for his quick release and patience with the *puck.* An 8-time *All-Star,* Sakic plays his best under the pressure of important games, helping lead the Avalanche to 2 *Stanley Cup* victories (1996, 2001). He took home the *Conn Smythe Trophy* as the *playoffs'* leading scorer in 1996, and was awarded the *Hart Trophy, Lady Byng Trophy* and the *Plus/Minus Award* for his efforts in 2001. Sakic also has excelled in international play as a gold medallist in the 1994 World Hockey Championship and as a member of Team Canada for the 1996 World Cup. One of the most respected players in the NHL, this soft-spoken leader has been his team's *captain* since 1990. Though nicknamed "Quoteless Joe" for his discomfort in formal settings, Sakic's ironic and mischievous sense of humor claims many victims.

SAWCHUK, TERRY: (G, HF, Top 50) Despite a right arm 2 inches shorter than his left (the result of a poorly healed break suffered in a rugby game), "Ukey" (for his Ukrainian heritage) became one of the greatest *goalies* in history. In 21 NHL seasons with the Detroit Red Wings (1950-55, 1957-64, 1968), Boston Bruins (1955-57), Toronto Maple Leafs (1964-67), Los Angeles Kings (1967) and the New York Rangers (1969 to his death off the ice in 1970), he won 5 *Stanley Cup* championships, won or shared the *Vezina Trophy* 4 times and was selected to the *All-Star Team* 7 times. When he won the

Calder Trophy in 1950-51, Sawchuk became the 1st player to win a *rookie* award in 3 different professional leagues (USHL in 1948 and *AHL* in 1949). In each of his first 5 seasons his *goals-against average* was less than 2.00. He went on to play more seasons, more games (971) and accumulate more *shutouts* (103) than any other goalie, and topped the list of all-time win leaders with 447 until *Patrick Roy* broke his record in 2000.

SELANNE, TEEMU: (F, A) This quick, strong skater with great instincts and a fast, accurate shot was a 3-sport athlete by the age of 10 (soccer, bandy and hockey). The "Finnish Flash" had an impressive NHL debut in 1992-93, winning the *Calder Trophy*, setting new *rookie* records for most *points* (132) and *goals* (76, led the NHL that year, 5th all-time), and being selected to the *All-Star Team*. His career continued to flourish with the Winnipeg Jets, Anaheim Ducks and San Jose Sharks. He has appeared in 7 consecutive *All-Star Games* since 1993, was the league's top scorer twice more (1998, and as the first recipient of the *Maurice "Rocket" Richard Award* in 1999), amassed 16 *hat tricks* in his first 8 seasons and was instrumental in Finland's 1998 Olympic bronze medal. Selanne, who was a kindergarten teacher in Finland for 3 years before joining the NHL, enjoys music, fishing and jogging, performs magic and card tricks and is an avid car collector (he has 25!)

SHORE, EDDIE: (D, HF, Top 50) This explosive player is generally regarded as the greatest and most feared *defenseman* of all time. He played 13½ seasons for the Boston Bruins starting in 1926, and is credited with leading that *franchise* to its first *Stanley Cup* (1929) and developing a loyal following for the team. Shore played his last ½ season with the New York Americans. In his 14-year career, Shore won the *Hart Trophy* 4 times (the only defenseman to do so), was voted to the *All-Star Team* 8 times, and won a 2nd Cup with the Bruins in 1939. In 1933, he was responsible for fracturing *Ace Bailey*'s skull and ending Bailey's hockey career. After he retired, Shore became a successful *AHL* team owner and manager with a reputation for being demanding but innovative. Shore died in 1985.

SUNDIN, MATS: (F, A) One of the dominant players on the world hockey stage, this *center* was the first European ever to be chosen first overall in a *draft* (1989 by the Quebec Nordiques). Four years after his 1990 debut, he was traded to the Toronto Maple Leafs where in 1997 he became the first European-born player ever to *captain* that team. Sundin is an offensive force with his fast skating, great stick-handling, and wide variety of shots including perhaps the best *backhand* in the NHL. Once banned from Swedish hockey for having abruptly departed to play in North America, Sundin has since participated in 3 World Cup Championship victories for Sweden (1991, 1992, 1998), one of only 3 players to have done so and the first since the 1960s. Today he is one of his country's most popular sportsman and an ambassador for Swedish hockey. This seven-time *All-Star* (1996-2002) has scored 30 or more *goals* in 8 of his 10 NHL seasons and has averaged over a *point* per game throughout his NHL career. Sundin, who is single, is also the honorary captain of the "Street Buds", the Leafs' ball hockey program for local youth.

VEZINA, GEORGES: (G, HF) He played with the *Montreal Canadiens* for 15 years from 1910-1925 in an era when *goalies* could not sprawl on the ice to *block* shots (the rule wasn't changed until 1922). The first goalie in NHL history to record a *shutout*, he helped the *Canadiens* win 2 NHA (National Hockey Association) championships, 3 NHL championships and 2 *Stanley Cups*. He played in his last game in November 1925 and died of tuberculosis four months later at the age of 39. The *Vezina Trophy* honoring the most outstanding goalie in the NHL is awarded annually in his memory.

YZERMAN, STEVE: (F, A) Capping a career of individual accomplishments, Yzerman led the Detroit Red Wings to 2 consecutive *Stanley Cup titles* (1997, 1998) after a 42-year drought, and then a 3rd in 2002. His 24 *points* in the 1998 *playoffs* led the NHL and earned him the *Conn Smythe Trophy*. Drafted by the Red Wings in 1983 at the tender age of 18, Yzerman is a rarity in today's NHL, having played with the same team his entire career. First named team *captain* in 1986 at age 21, he is the longest-serving captain in NHL history. This *center* went on to score 1,000 *points* in fewer games than any other player except *Wayne Gretzky*, and is currently 3rd among active players and 6th all-time with 1,662 points. Yzerman had 6 consecutive 100+ point seasons (1987-1993, including 155 points in 1988-89), five 50+ *goal* seasons and played in 10 *All-Star Games*. In addition to being a sensational skater, effective *penalty killer*, and gritty leader willing to sacrifice his body, Yzerman is known for being modest and kind off the ice where he enjoys time with his wife and 3 daughters.

GLOSSARY

Please check the Index if you don't find what you are looking for here.

Adams Division: with the *Patrick Division* made up the *Wales Conference* until the 1992-93 season; renamed the *Northeast Division* of the *Eastern Conference* starting with the 1993-94 season.

All-Star Game: a mid-season *exhibition game* pitting selected stars of North American origin against selected stars from the rest of the world; from 1969 to 1997, the game was played between representatives from the *NHL*'s two *conferences*.

All-Star Team: the best *NHL* players at each position, selected at the end of each season by the Professional Hockey Writers' Association; 12 players are chosen, 2 for each of the 6 player positions (divided into First-Team and Second-Team All-Stars); they do not actually play together in a game.

assist: the *pass* or passes which immediately precede a successful scoring attempt; a maximum of two assists are credited for one *goal*.

attacking zone: the area between the opponents' *blue line* and their *goal*.

backcheck: an attempt by a player, on his way back to his *defending zone*, to regain the *puck* from the opposition or slow them down by *checking* or harassing an opponent who has the puck.

backhand shot: a shot or *pass* made with the *stick* from the left side by a right-handed player or from the right side by a left-handed player.

beat the defense: to get by one or both of the *defensemen*.

beat the goalie: to outwit the *goalie* and score a *goal*.

behind the net: the area of ice behind the *goal cage*.

blind pass: to pass the *puck* without looking.

blue lines: two blue, 12-inch wide lines running parallel across the ice, each 60 feet from the *goal line*, that are used in determining *offsides* and *icing*; they divide the *rink* into three *zones* called the *attacking, defending* and *neutral* (or center) *zones*; the *defending blue line* is the line closer to a player's own *net*; the *attacking blue line* is the one farther from his net.

boarding or board-checking: a *minor penalty* which occurs when a player uses any method (*body checking, elbowing* or *tripping*) to throw an opponent violently into the *boards*; if an injury is caused, it becomes a *major penalty*.

boards or board wall: a wooden or fiberglass wall 3 ½ to 4 feet high which surrounds the *rink* to keep the *puck* and players from accidentally leaving the rink and injuring spectators; all rinks have shatterproof glass that rises above the boards to provide additional protection.

body check: when a player bumps or slams into an opponent with either his hip or shoulder (the only legal moves) to block his progress or throw him off-balance; only allowed against an opponent in control of the *puck* or against the last player to control it immediately after he gives it up.

break: a chance to start a *rush* when the opposing *forwards* are caught out of position.

breakaway or breakout: a fast break in which an attacker with the *puck* skates in alone on the *goalie*, having gotten past or clear of the *defensemen*.

breaking pass: a pass to a teammate who is trying for a *breakaway*.

butt-ending: a *major penalty* which occurs when a player jabs an opponent with the shaft of his hockey stick.

butterfly style: a *goaltender* playing style in which the goalie often goes down to the ice knees-first to stop shots, with his knees together but feet out so his entire leg pads face front; this configuration, which resembles a butterfly, is more popular today because it provides greater coverage against the more frequent low shots; compare to *standup style* and *hybrid style*.

Campbell Conference: was one of the two conferences in the *NHL* that contained the *Norris* and *Smythe Divisions* until 1992-93; renamed the *Western Conference* in 1993.

carom: a rebound of the *puck* off the *boards* or any other object.

center or center forward: the center player in the *forward line* who usually leads his team's attack when they are trying to score a *goal*; he takes part in most of the *face-offs*; he controls the *puck* and tries to score or *pass* it to a teammate who is in a better position to score a goal.

center face-off circle: a circle, measuring 30 feet in diameter, at the center of the ice where the *puck* is dropped in a *face-off* to start the game and to restart the game after a *goal* has been scored.

center ice: the area between the two *blue lines*, also called the *neutral zone*.

centering pass: a pass from an attacking player towards the middle of the ice to a teammate with a better angle to shoot at the *goal*.

center line: a red 12-inch wide line across the ice, midway between the two *goals*.

charging: a *minor penalty* called against a player who makes a deliberate move of more than two steps when *body checking* an opponent; if serious injury is caused or blood is drawn it becomes a *major penalty* and a *game misconduct*.

check or checking: any contact initiated by a defending player against an opponent to get the *puck* away from him or slow him down; there are two main types of *checks*: *stick check* and *body check*; these are only allowed against a player in control of the puck or against the last player to control it immediately after he gives it up; checking after too many steps or strides becomes *charging*.

clearing the puck: getting the *puck* out of one's own *defending zone*.

clearing the zone: when a defending player sends the *puck* out of the opponent's *attacking zone*, all the attacking players must leave or *clear* the zone to avoid being called *offsides* when the puck reenters the zone.

cover: when a player stays close to an opponent to prevent him from receiving a *pass* or making a play on offense.

crease lines: the red lines that form the semi-circular area with a 6-foot radius in front of the *goal* called the *goal crease*.

cross bar: the horizontal bar that connects the top of the two *goalposts*.

cross-checking: a *minor penalty* which occurs when a player holds his *stick* in both hands and drives the shaft into an opponent; if serious injury is caused or blood is drawn it becomes a *major penalty* and a *game misconduct*.

dead puck: a *puck* that flies out of the *rink*, is *frozen* or that a player has caught in his hand; play is stopped and then re-started with a *face-off*.

defending zone: the *zone* or area nearest the *goal* a team is defending.

defensemen: two players who make up a team's defensive unit, usually stationed in or near their *defending zone* to help the *goalie* guard against attack; sometimes they lead an attack. The left *defenseman* covers the left half of the *rink*, the right defenseman plays to the right, but they can skate into each other's territory.

defensive line: consists of both *defensemen*.

deflection: causing any *pass* or shot to stray from its intended course; a shot or pass that hits an object such as a *stick* or *skate* and goes into the *net* for a score; when a *goalie* bats away a *puck* shot at him.

deke or deking: a decoying or faking motion by the puck carrier; the art of making a defensive player think you are going to *pass* or move in a certain direction when you are not; there are *shoulder dekes, stick dekes* and *head dekes*.

delay of game: a *minor penalty* imposed on any player who purposely delays the game in any way, such as by shooting or batting the *puck* outside the playing area or displacing a *goalpost* from its normal position.

delayed penalty: a penalty against a team that has only 4 players on the ice, assessed only when one of its players gets out of the *penalty box*.

delayed whistle or delayed call: when an *official* raises his arm but does not blow his whistle, waiting to see the outcome of a play before calling a *penalty*; this is done so as not to penalize the non-offending team by stopping its momentum.

double minor: a type of *minor penalty* given for certain accidental infractions that result in an *injury* to another player or for certain deliberate attempts to injure an opponent that are unsuccessful; penalty time of 4 minutes is served, double the time of a normal minor penalty.

draw: *face-off*.

drop pass: when a player simply leaves the *puck* behind for a teammate following him.

Eastern Conference: the renamed *Wales Conference* beginning with the 1993-94 season which contains the *Atlantic, Northeast* and *Southeast Divisions*.

elbowing: a *minor penalty* which occurs when a player strikes his opponent with an elbow to impede his progress.

empty-net goal: a *goal* scored against a team that has *pulled the goalie*.

endboards: the *boards* at each end of the *rink*.

enforcer: also called the *policeman*, he is usually the most penalized player on a team; he has the job of protecting his teammates from harm; generally a larger player who is not afraid of any fight.

exhibition game: a game not included in the *regular-season* schedule and which does not count in the *standings*; the *All-Star Game* or games played before the season begins.

expansion: the addition of teams to the *NHL*.

expansion draft: a special arrangement to assist new *franchises* in obtaining players where *expansion teams* choose unprotected players from other teams' *rosters*.

expansion team: a team that has been recently added to the *NHL*.

face mask: the protective mask worn by the *goalie*.

face-off: the method of starting play; the dropping of the *puck* by the *official* between the *sticks* of two opposing players standing one stick length apart with stick blades flat on the ice; used to begin each *period* or to resume play when it has stopped for other reasons; also known as the *draw* or the drop.

face-off circles and spots: the various circular spots on the ice where an *official* and two players will hold a *face-off* to begin or to resume the action of the game; there is one blue face-off circle and four red face-off spots located in the *neutral zone*; two red face-off circles are found at each end of the ice.

falling on the puck: a *minor penalty* which occurs when a player other than the *goalie* closes his hand on the *puck*, deliberately falls on the puck, or gathers the puck under his body while lying on the ice.

feeding: passing the *puck* to a teammate.

fighting: a *major penalty* which occurs when two or more players drop their *sticks* and *gloves* and fight; if a *referee* deems one player to be the instigator, that player also receives a *minor penalty* and a *misconduct penalty*; the minor penalty for a less severe pushing and shoving match is called *roughing*.

flat pass: when a player *passes* the *puck* to a teammate along the surface of the ice.

flip pass: a *pass* by a player to a teammate that lifts the *puck* from the ice and sends it through the air, usually for the purpose of getting it over an opponent's *stick*.

flip shot: a shot in which a player cups the *puck* in his *stick* blade, then flips it with his wrists up off the ice towards the *goal*; this sometimes makes the puck harder to block.

forecheck: to *check* or harass an opponent who has the *puck* in his *defending zone* and keep the opponents in their end of the *rink* while trying to regain control of the puck; usually done by the *forwards*.

forehand: a shot or pass taken from the right side of a right-handed player or from the left side of a left-handed player.

forward line: also known as the attacking line, it consists of two *wings* (*right* and *left*) and a *center*; these three players play nearest the opponent's *goal* and are responsible for most of the scoring.

forwards: the three players who make up the attacking line or *forward line* of a team — the *center* and the *right* and *left wings*.

foul: any infraction of the rules that will draw a *penalty*.

4-on-4: when each team plays with 4 *skaters* plus a *goalie*, one less skater per side than in a standard hockey game.

franchise: a team; the legal arrangement that establishes ownership of a team.

freeze the puck: to hold the *puck* against the *boards* with the *skate* or *stick* in order to stop play briefly or gain a *face-off*.

full strength: when a team has its full complement of 6 players on the ice, normally 5 *skaters* plus a *goalie*.

get the jump: to move fast and thereby get a good start on the opponents.

goal: provides one *point*; scored when a *puck* entirely crosses the red *goal line* between the *goalposts* and beneath the *crossbar*; also the informal term used to refer to the area consisting of the goalposts and the *net* guarded by the *goalie* into which a puck must enter to score a point.

goal cage: a 6 foot wide by 4 foot high tubular steel frame consisting of a *cross bar* and two *goalposts* to which a *net* is attached.

goal crease: a semi-circular area with a 6 foot radius in front of the opening of the *goal*; denotes the playing area of the *goaltender* within which attacking players must not obstruct his movement or vision.

goal line: the two-inch red line between the *goalposts* that stretches in both directions to the *sideboards*.

goalkeeper, goalie or goaltender: the heavily padded player who guards the *goal*; prevents opponents from scoring by stopping the *puck* any way he can.

goalposts: the metal bars which rest on the center of the *goal line*, between which a *puck* must pass to score a *goal*; the frame to which the *net* is attached.

hat trick: three or more *goals* scored by a player in a single game.

head deke: when a player drops his head as though moving one way and quickly moves in another to fake out the opponent.

high-sticking: a *minor penalty* which occurs when a player carries his *stick* above the normal height of his opponent's shoulders and hits or menaces the opponent with it; if *injury* is caused it becomes a *major penalty*; if a *referee* determines that the raising of the stick was unintentional and no contact occurred, it is considered a team infraction, and a *face-off* is held in the offender's *defensive zone*.

holding: a *minor penalty* which occurs when a player grabs and holds onto an opponent (or his *stick*) with his hands or arms to impede the opponent's progress.

holding the puck: see *falling on the puck*.

home team: the team in whose arena the game is being played; the team wearing the lighter uniforms.

hook check: a sweep of the *stick* low to the ice to take the *puck* from an opponent's stick.

hooking: a *minor penalty* which occurs when a player attempts to impede the progress of another player by hooking any part of the opponent's body with the blade of his *stick*.

hybrid style: a *goaltender* playing style that combines *butterfly style* (for low shots) and *standup style* (for high shots).

icing: a violation which occurs when the team in possession of the *puck* shoots it from behind the red *center line* across the opponent's *goal line* into the end of the *rink* (but not into the *goal*) and a member of the opposing team touches it first; results in a *face-off* in the offender's *defending zone*; a *shorthanded* team cannot be called for icing.

interference: a *penalty* in hockey called when a player attempts to impede the motion of an opponent not in possession of the *puck*.

intermission: a 15-minute recess between each of the three *periods* of a game.

kneeing: a *minor penalty* which occurs when a player uses a knee to hit his opponent in the leg, thigh or lower body.

lead pass: a *pass* sent ahead of a moving teammate designed to meet the player at the location he is headed.

lie: angle made by the shaft of the *stick* and the blade.

line change: when the entire *forward line* and / or *defensive line* are replaced at once; puts players on the ice who work well together.

linesmen: the two *officials* on the ice, one positioned toward each end of the *rink*, responsible for calling *offsides* at the *blue lines* or *center line* and any *icing* violations; they conduct most of the *face-offs*, call *minor penalties*, sometimes advise the *referees* concerning penalties, and separate players who are *fighting*; they wear black pants and an official league sweater, and are on *skates*.

major penalty: a type of individual *penalty* called for more serious infractions of the rules; 5 minutes in duration whether or not the non-penalized team scores.

match-up: a pairing of players on opposing teams who will *cover* each other during the hockey game.

minor penalty: a type of *penalty* lasting 2 minutes; if the non-penalized team scores a *power play goal* during this time, the penalty ends immediately and the penalized player returns to the ice.

National Hockey League (NHL): a professional league started on November 22, 1917; currently contains 30 teams in the U.S. and Canada.

net: the *goal*; netting attached to the *goalposts* and frame of the goal to trap the *puck* when a goal is scored.

neutral zone: the area at mid-ice between the *blue lines*.

Norris Division: with the *Smythe Division* made up the *Campbell Conference* until the 1992-93 season; renamed the *Central Division* of the *Western Conference* in 1993.

officials: two *referees* and two *linesmen* on the ice calling infractions and handing out *penalties* plus several off-ice *officials* including two *goal judges*, the *game timekeeper*, the *penalty timekeeper*, the *official scorer*, the *statistician* and the *video goal judge*.

offside: a violation which occurs when both *skates* of an attacking player cross the opponent's *blue line* before the *puck* is passed or carried into the *attacking zone*; also called when a player passes the puck from his *defending zone* to a teammate across the red *center line* (*two-line pass*); this is one of the most common calls made in a hockey game and results in a *face-off*.

offside pass: see *two-line pass*.

on-the-fly: making player changes or *substitutions* while play is under way.

on the road: when an *NHL* team plays games away from its home arena.

open ice: the part of the ice that is free of opponents.

overtime: an additional *period* used to break a *tie*; see *sudden-death*.

overtime loss: the result for a team that loses a game in *overtime* that was tied after *regulation*; this category was created starting with the 1999-2000 season and is worth 1 *point* in the *standings*.

passing: when one player uses his *stick* to send the *puck* to a teammate.

passout: a *pass* by an attacking player from behind his opponent's *net* or *goal line* to a teammate in front of the net.

Patrick Division: with the *Adams Division* made up the *Wales Conference* until the 1992-93 season; renamed the *Atlantic Division* of the *Eastern Conference* in 1993.

penalty: punishment of a player for a violation of the rules, resulting in suspension from the game for a period of time; 6 types exist: *minor, bench, major, misconduct, match* and *goalkeeper penalties*.

penalty box: an area with a *bench* just off the ice, behind the *sideboards* outside the playing area, where penalized players serve their *penalty* time.

penalty killer: a player expert at *backchecking* and keeping or gaining control of the *puck* under difficult circumstances who is trained to diffuse a *power play* when his team is *shorthanded*.

penalty shot: a free shot awarded a player who was illegally interfered with, preventing him from a clear scoring opportunity; the shot is taken with only the *goalie* guarding against it.

periods: three 20-minute playing intervals separated by two *intermissions*; also refers to any *overtime*.

points: the left and right positions taken by the *defensemen* of the attacking team, just inside the *blue line* of the *attacking zone*; also the term used to describe the defensemen playing at this location; also an individual statistic for players, equal to their *goals* plus *assists*; also a team statistic used to determine team *standings* (2 points for each win and 1 point for each tie or *overtime loss* during the *regular season*).

poke check: a quick jab or thrust with the *stick* at the *puck* or opponent's stick to knock the puck away from him.

policeman: see *enforcer.*

power play: an attack by a team at *full strength* against a team playing one man (or two men) *shorthanded* because of a *penalty* (or penalties) which resulted in a player on the opposing team receiving *penalty-box* time.

puck: a black, vulcanized rubber disc used to play hockey, 1 inch thick and 3 inches in diameter, weighing between 5 ½ and 6 ounces; it is frozen to prevent excessive bouncing and changed throughout the game; can travel up to 120 miles per hour on a *slap shot.*

pulling the goalie: taking the *goalkeeper* off the ice and replacing him with a *forward*; leaves the *goal* unguarded so is only used as a desperate last minute attempt to score.

ragging: retaining the *puck* by clever stickhandling; often used by a *shorthanded* team to kill time.

rebound: a *puck* that bounces off the *goalie's* body or equipment.

red line: the line that divides the length of the ice surface in half.

referees: the two chief *officials* in a hockey game, distinguished from the other officials by a red armband; they start the game, call most of the *penalties* and make the final decision in any dispute; they are responsible for making sure the ice, the *nets* and the clock are in good condition; they wear black pants and an official league sweater; they are also on *skates.*

referees' crease: a semi-circular area, with a 10-foot radius, marked in red on the ice in front of the *timekeepers'* bench into which players may not follow a *referee.*

rink: the iced area inside the *boards* on which the game of hockey is played; it is 200 feet long by 85 feet wide with rounded corners.

rockered blades: used by professional ice hockey skaters; the gentle curve in the blade of an ice *skate* produced by rounding the toe and heel of the blade to make it easier for hockey players to turn quickly.

roster: a list of the players on a team.

roughing: a *minor penalty* for a pushing or shoving altercation; a less severe penalty than *fighting.*

rush: an individual or combined attack by a team in possession of the *puck.*

save: the act of a *goalie* in blocking or stopping a shot at the *goal.*

scramble: several players from both sides close together battling for possession of the *puck*.

screen shot: a shot on *goal* that the *goalie* cannot see because it was taken from behind one or more players from either team standing in front of the *net*.

seam: a gap in the *defense* between two or more defending players.

shooting angle: the angle determined by the position of the shooting player in relation to the *goal* at the moment he shoots the *puck*.

shorthanded: a team with one or more players off the ice in the *penalty box* when the opponent has its full complement of 6 players; also a *power play* for the other team.

shot on goal (SOG): a scoring attempt that would enter the *goal* if not stopped by a *goalie*; results in either a *goal* or a *save*.

shoulder deke: a quick move of the shoulder in one direction and the player in another to fake out the opponent.

sideboards: the *boards* along the sides of the *rink*.

skaters: players who move around the *rink* during play, generally everyone on a team except the *goalie*.

slap shot: a shot in which the player raises his *stick* in a backswing, with his strong hand held low on the shaft and his other hand on the end as a pivot; as the stick comes down toward the *puck*, the player leans into the stick to put all his power behind the shot and add velocity to the puck; achieves an extremely high speed (up to 120 miles per hour) but is usually less accurate than a *wrist shot*.

slashing: a *minor penalty* which occurs when a player swings his *stick* hard at an opponent, whether or not contact is made; if injury is caused it becomes a *major penalty* and a *game misconduct*.

sleeper: an attacking player who slips into the center or *neutral zone* behind the attacking *defensemen*; same as a floater or a hanger.

slot: the area directly in front of the *goal*, between the *face-off circles*; most *goals* are scored on shots taken from this area.

slow whistle: when an *official* waits to blow his whistle because of a *delayed offside* or *delayed penalty* call.

Smythe Division: with the *Norris Division* made up the *Campbell Conference* until the 1992-93 season; renamed the *Pacific Division* of the *Western Conference* in 1993.

solo: a *rush* by a player without assistance from a teammate.

spearing: a *major penalty* which occurs when a player jabs, or even just attempts to jab, the point of his *stick* blade into another player's body; one of the most serious infractions a player can commit; results in an automatic *game misconduct*.

standup style: in this older style of goaltending, the *goalie* rarely goes down to the ice knees-first to stop shots, but rather just puts his pads together to stop low shots; when he does go down, he kneels with the lower half of his pads on the ice. Compare to *butterfly style* and *hybrid style*.

stick deke: when a player's *stick* is moved as though for a shot, but instead the player moves the *puck* past the defending player; done to fake out the opponent.

stickhandling: moving the *puck* along the ice with the *stick* blade.

substitution: occurs when a player comes off the *bench* to replace a player coming out of the game; can be made at any time and play does not need to stop.

sudden-death overtime: an *overtime period* that ends as soon as one team scores a *goal*, determining the winner and terminating the game.

sweep check: a *check* made by a player with one hand on the *stick* and one knee so low it is practically on the ice, with the shaft and blade of the stick flat on the ice to sweep the *puck* away from an opponent.

third-man-in rule: the third man in a fight gets a *game misconduct penalty* and is out of the game for its duration, even if he was only trying to break it up; created to discourage players from jumping into a fight.

thread the needle: to *pass* the *puck* to a teammate through a narrow gap in a crowd of players.

three-on-one: a type of *break* with three attackers skating in on one *defenseman*; this is a desperate situation for the defense.

three-on-two: a type of *break* with three attacking players skating against two defensive players.

title: championship.

trailer: a player who follows his teammate on the attack, seemingly out of the action but actually in a position to receive a *drop pass*.

tripping: a *minor penalty* which occurs when a player places his *stick* or a part of his body under or around the feet or legs of an opponent, causing him to lose his balance; will also be called if a player kicks an opponent's *skates* out from under him.

two-line pass: a type of *offside* violation occurring when a player passes the *puck* from his *defending zone* to a teammate across the red *center line*; play is stopped for a *face-off*; also known as an *offside pass*.

two-on-one: a type of *break* with two attacking players skating against one defensive player.

two-on-two: a type of *break* with two attacking players skating against two defensive players.

under-led pass: a *pass* behind or to one side of a teammate, making it difficult for him to control the *puck*.

veteran: experienced player.

waffle pad: a large rectangular pad attached to the front of the *goalie's* *stick* hand; also called a blocking *glove*.

Wales Conference: was one of the two conferences in the *NHL* consisting of the *Patrick* and *Adams Divisions* until the 1992-93 season; renamed the *Eastern Conference* in 1993.

wash out: a *goal* that is ruled invalid by a *referee*, or the "waving off" of an infraction called by the *linesmen*.

Western Conference: the renamed *Campbell Conference* beginning with the 1993-94 season which contains the *Central, Northwest* and *Pacific Divisions*.

wings: two players who flank the *center* on his right and left sides and who, with him, make up the attacking line or *forward line*.

wrist shot: a shot made using a strong flicking of the wrist and forearm muscles, with the *stick* blade kept on the ice; it is slower but usually more accurate than a *slap shot*.

Zamboni: the brand of machine used to clean or "flood" the ice.

zones: three areas made up by the two *blue lines*; the *attacking zone* is the area farthest from the *goal* a player is defending; the *neutral zone* is the central area; the *defending zone* is the area where a player's goal is located (the goal where his team's *goalie* is stationed).

INDEX

Bolded page numbers indicate a photograph, diagram or table.

OFFICIALS' HAND SIGNALS

BOARDING: pounding a closed fist into the open palm of the opposite hand (see page 42).

CHARGING: clenched fists rotating around each other in front of the chest (see page 42).

CROSS-CHECKING: two clenched fists extending out from the chest in a forward and backward motion (see page 42, 43).

DELAYED WHISTLE OR CALLING OF PENALTY: one arm extended up in the air by the *referee* with whistle in mouth, then pointing once to the guilty player (see page 41).

ELBOWING: tapping the elbow with the opposite hand (see page 42).

HIGH-STICKING: both hands clenched, held one just above the other at forehead level (see page 43).

HOLDING: clasping one wrist with the other hand, just in front of the chest (see page 43).

123

HOOKING: tugging motion with both arms, as though pulling something toward himself (see page 44).

ICING: arms folded against the chest (see page 34).

INTERFERENCE: fists closed with arms crossed and stationary in front of the chest (see page 44).

KNEEING: slapping the knee with one hand, both skates on the ice (see page 44).

MISCONDUCT: both hands placed on the hips, then pointing to the penalized player (see page 38-39).

OFFSIDES: *linesman* points at the *blue line* (see page 32-33).

ROUGHING, FIGHTING: a thrusting motion of the arm extending from the side (see page 44, 43).

124

SLASHING: a chopping motion with the edge of one hand on the opposite forearm (see page 45).

SLOW WHISTLE: a *linesman's* non-whistle arm held straight up; lowered the instant the *puck* crosses the *blue line* back into the *neutral zone* (see page 33).

SPEARING: a jabbing motion with both hands in front of the body (see page 45).

TRIPPING: hitting right leg with right hand below the knee, both skates on the ice (see page 45).

WASH-OUT (REFEREE): both arms swung laterally across the body with palms facing down to disallow a *goal*.

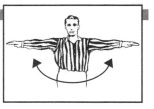

WASH-OUT (LINESMEN): both arms swung laterally across the shoulders with palms facing down when there is no *icing* or no *offsides*.

UNSPORTSMANLIKE CONDUCT: using both hands to form the letter T in front of the chest (see page 38).

ORDER FORM

Order any of the following Spectator Guides:

Title	Qty	Price	Total
Basketball Made Simple, 3rd ed.		$11.95	
Football Made Simple, 4th ed.		$11.95	
Ice Hockey Made Simple, 4th ed.		$11.95	
Soccer Made Simple		$11.95	
		Subtotal	
Add $2.99 plus $0.99 per book for shipping & handling →		S&H	
		Sales Tax (in CA only)	
		Total	

Order on the Internet at: **www.firstbasesports.com**
or
Mail this form to :

First Base Sports, Inc.
P.O. Box 1731
Manhattan Beach, CA 90267-1731

Name _____

Street Address _____

City _____

State _____ Zip _____

Phone No. _____

Method of Payment:

Check ❑   Money Order ❑